Enriching Primary Schooling in India

Enriching Primary Schooling in India

L.C. Singh
Meenu Dev

SHIPRA

Rs. 800

ISBN: 978-81-7541-782-3

First Published in India in 2015

Enriching Primary Schooling in India

Published by:

SHIPRA PUBLICATIONS
LG 18-19, Pankaj Central Market,
I.P. Ext., Patparganj, Delhi 110092, India
Ph.: 011- 2223 5152, 2223 6152
Email: info@shiprapublication.com
www.shiprapublication.com

Preface

'If you want to be somebody, Grow' so says the great German philosopher, Goethe, as the golden prescription for education at all levels of schooling, the basic aim of education being to help every individual grow to the optimum of one's potentials. A wonderful idea, very close to the Indian philosophy of education down the ages verily reflected and reverberated even today not only in the thought process of contemporary Indian educators like Gandhi, Vivekanand, Aurobindo, as the underpinning of all the post-independence era Commissions, but also as the policy documents on education. Yet, at the ground reality, the grand ideal seems to have been suffering from a kind of tragic flaw, the Sin of Acedia, or the sense of despair all the while, even to reach the bare goal of 'Education for All', despite all the good intentions, innovations and remedial measures opted to that end over the recent decades of educational planning and implementation by the whole lot of formal institutions and non-formal as well as informal agencies country-wide. Maybe, the enormity of the problem of illiteracy, of education of the out-of-school children and, for that matter, of the school drop-outs, may have dwindled to quite an extent, its deep-seatedness in the socio-economic milieu and cultural bias does appear to have baffled and belied most of the efforts and concerns involved to ameliorate their predicament.

The purpose of this volume is to enrich the primary schooling. It is not only to highlight the gravity of the problems of out-of-school and drop-out children and the various strategies adopted to help the cause of their education through formal, non-formal and informal ways, but also to suggest how teachers, teacher educators and other stakeholders in the society at large can contribute to tackle the question of mainstreaming them as an integral part of the education system *per se*, individually as well as collectively. It aims at improving the overall quality of primary schooling in the country.

With profound regards, we express our warm thanks to the vast galaxy of our professional friends and colleagues for their willing and prompt cooperation and consultations provided in the drafting of this book, which is primarily addressed to building a congenial environment for the teachers, teacher educators and other stakeholders, particularly in teacher education to promote the cause of inclusive education of the out-of-school children in the challenging perspective of the system of education at the elementary level.

We specially place on record our sincere gratitude to Prof. Jogender K. Bhatia, JMI; Dr. Usha Sharma, NCERT; Dr. Sudarshan Mishra, RCU; Dr. Sharda, DIET, New Delhi; Dr. S. K. Rout, RCU; Dr. Anshu Agrawal, Lingayat University; and Ms. R. Garima, MBC, Delhi for their valuable contributions in the form of brief snippets, clippings and write-ups on revamping of primary schooling, specifically crucial aspects of the issue of out-of-school children to bring them in the mainstream during the last couple of decades. Their interventions have really gone a long way in enhancing not only the content and its pedagogical aspects, but also in underlining the intent and scope of the theme reflected in this work. Hence, our honest appreciation and acknowledgement for their meaningful inputs to help facilitate the building of an approach that could be tangible to realize the end goal, as smoothly as feasible in the immediate context of primary schooling.

We also thank Dr. D. N. Khosla for pruning the text and making it press-worthy through thorough-going editorial inputs to shape it the way it is being presented as an academic-cum-research document to help researchers, teachers and scholars as well as lay readers to understand the *leit motif* of this piece of work, and enjoy going through it as an humble attempt to boost schooling for all, in a nearly comprehensive way, specially in the context of bringing more and more out-of-school children to the mainstreaming process in pursuit of all inclusive primary schools.

This title stands dedicated to the cause of building a knowledge society, where everybody has a free and fair chance to 'Grow', to be 'Somebody', in the long run.

New Delhi

Prof. L.C. Singh
Dr. Meenu Dev

Contents

1

Out-of-School Children

Early education is the foundation of the later learning process. Early learning creates more learning.

—Dr James Heckman*

It has been well said that a tree inclines the way its early twig bends. Early investment in a child's future, likewise, is said to pay ten times more in one's later part of life. In India, elementary education has been given high priority both by the Central and the State governments with a number of inputs in place to ensure the participation of all children to have quality education. The access to school expanded with investment on different aspects like (i) physical infrastructure including school building, functional toilets, safe drinking water, child-friendly classrooms, play fields, etc; and (ii) human resources including appointment of teachers, non-teaching staff and other educational administrators, involving School Management Committee (SMC), parents, community members and other stakeholders as active collaborators in the functioning of the school. At long last, after the 1950 declaration of the Directive Principles of State Policy and Universal Education, free and compulsory elementary education has been a constitutional right made fundamental as per Right of Children to Free and Compulsory Education Act (RTE) 2009. Despite the Education for

---

* Nobel Laureate in Economics; Expert in Economics of Human Development.

All (EFA) campaign and DPEP efforts for quite a while and with eight million children never having stepped inside a school and 80 million having dropped out without completing basic schooling over the years, the United Nations Children's Fund found the situation like a national emergency. It called for equipping the government and civil society to implement the Right to Education Act, 2009 in letter and spirit. The Act also aims to further increase enrolment and take forward the government's goal of achieving universal elementary education. Sarva Shiksha Abhiyan (SSA) forms the government scheme for launching Universal Elementary Education (UEE), with majority of our schools covered under it.

Over the years, there has, of course, been a significant quantitative expansion of elementary schools in the country. Access and enrolment at the primary stage of education having reached near universal levels, as many as 11.18 million more children had been enrolled in the last three years. Even though gender disparity in enrolment across social groups has gone down, this did not help much in controlling the drop-out rate. It came down marginally to 27 per cent at the primary level and 41 per cent at the elementary level. Worse, 13 per cent of students did not transit from primary to the upper primary level. There was not much on offer for migrant children and drop-outs, who wanted to rejoin school, though the Act did provide for bridge courses. With regard to pupil-teacher ratio (PTR), while the average PTR had improved across most States between the academic years 2011-12 and 2012-13, the percentage of schools with adverse PTR was still high, indicating that redeployment of teachers was needed, in addition to recruitment of qualified and better trained teachers, which would also improve the learning outcomes.

The gender gap in elementary education narrowed and the percentage of children belonging to scheduled castes and scheduled tribes enrolled in proportion to their population, yet, the goal of universal elementary education continued to elude. There remained an unfinished agenda of universal education, particularly at the upper primary stage. The number of children, particularly children from disadvantaged groups and weaker sections, who dropped out of school before completing upper primary education, has remained high. The quality of learning achievement has not always been entirely satisfactory even in the case of children, who completed the elementary education. Being still unable to retain children in schools, the high drop-out rates and low attendance have become major challenges in achieving the UEE goals.

The Moot Point

Such a situation calls for reviewing the nature and psychology of out-of-school children; providing initiatives at the government and non-government levels for school improvement; and providing quality education to these children. It is high time to provide education for the integration of these children into the mainstream; for effective pedagogical interventions and evaluation of learning outcomes; and orientation of primary school teachers to enable them to look after these children with affection, love and care.

Out-of-School Children (OSC): Concept and Nature

The concept of out-of-school children can be understood in terms of their following categories. First, those children, who left school due to weak performance in lower classes, resulting into hardship in their further studies; second, those children, who have never been to school; and third, those children, who were engaged in child labour and were migrants.

The nature of out-of-school children is, by and large, such that children, who have dropped out once, are always at the risk of dropping out again. Such children need extra attention and a feeling that they are welcome in the school. The sense of belongingness to the classroom and the school community is considered a necessary prerequisite for a successful school at the primary stage. This is critical for the sustainable development of such children in school, especially at the elementary level.

Characteristics of Out-of-School Children

Among other factors, most of the out-of-school children seem to have displayed the following traits:

- Had enrolled themselves, but later dropped out.

- Had never been to school.
- May have dropped out to work or to get married.
- Migration may also have been one of the reasons.
- Dropped out due to unfavourable school environment.
- Dropped out as they could not adjust in the rigid school system.
- Could not show a desired level of achievement.
- Had run away due to fear of the teacher

Demographic Classification of Out-of-School Children

The out-of-school children generally belong to certain specific sections of society such as:

1. Geographical Area
   - Plain
   - Hilly
   - Coastal
   - Tribal belt
   - Desert
2. Urban/Rural Residential Location
   - Village
   - Urbanised village
   - City
   - Town
3. Socio-Cultural Parental Background
   - Literate
   - Illiterate
   - Farmers
   - Farm labour
   - Urban slum dwellers
4. Reservation Category
   - Schedule Caste
   - Schedule Tribe
   - Other Backward Classes (OBC)
   - Below Poverty Line (BPL)
   - Economically Weaker Sections of Society (EWS)
   - Religious Minority (weaker sections)

5. Others
   - Child labourers
   - Rag pickers
   - Orphans

Early Mainstreaming Initiatives

Mainstreaming strategies for out-of-school children can be broadly divided into three major drives: (i) enrolment; (ii) universalising physical access; and (iii) alternative and innovative education provisions.

Enrolment Drive

Enrolment in a school, wherever available, is the first step towards mainstreaming the out-of-school children. Enrolment drives under different names and nature are carried out in different states with the objectives of: generating awareness about the mission; sensitising the masses about out-of-school children; identifying children, who are not in school; and enrolling them for schooling. The elected leaders from the district, block and panchayat levels participate in enrolment drives conducted by the State Sarva Shiksha Abhiyans (SSAs). They visit houses and talk to parents of out-of-school children. Such children are encouraged to participate in various cultural and sports activities and then enrolled in formal schools with fanfare. The enrolment drives create a congenial environment to push forward the Mission's objectives of universal elementary education and, in the process, involve all stakeholders from every strata of the society.

Universal Access

Providing universal access to elementary education is the foremost objective under SSA. Unserved areas are provided with primary and elementary schools under DPEP (District Primary Education Programme) and later SSA to achieve this objective. But still, there remain the unreached, scattered and remote habitations in the country, where the facilities of elementary schooling are not yet accessible. As per the Seventh All India School Education Survey (NCERT, 2006), as many as 86.97 per cent habitations are served by primary schools. Of these, 53 per cent habitations have primary schools located within the respective habitations and 34 per cent within one km radius. Likewise, 78.12 per cent habitations of the country have upper primary schools within the respective habitations or within a distance of three kms. The initiation of Education Guarantee Scheme (EGS) became instrumental in providing additional access to schooling in many of the unserved, scattered and remote habitations. The EGS centre usually has one teacher for every 30-40 children and an additional teacher is provided when the number of children increases beyond 40. Establishing EGS centres is a community-initiated and locally-managed temporary facility, before providing permanent schooling facilities to the unserved habitations. In 2005-06, over 1.11 lakh EGS centres provided educational facilities to over 40.42 lakh children.

Alternative and Innovative Education Provisions

Since the days of DPEP, diverse strategies have been adopted under the alternative and innovative education schemes to facilitate the process of mainstreaming of out-of-school children. With the inception of SSA in the year 2001 to provide education for all, the scope and range of applying these strategies widened so as to achieve the mammoth mandate of enrolling each child of the country in a regular school or provide an alternative arrangement of an equivalent quality.

A few innovative initiatives, as discussed below, may serve as bold inputs in this context.

Case Study: Mamidipudi Venkatarangaiya Foundation (MVF), Andhra Pradesh

The MVF model aimed at eliminating child labour through the universalisation of quality formal education and working towards the creation of awareness and demand for education among the poor. Operationalized in Ranga Reddy district of Andhra Pradesh in 1991 with universalization of formal primary education as one of its key objectives, MVF maintains that each and every child is a potential worker. Its programmes, therefore, target all children, believing that every child going to school means keeping the child away from working. Providing schooling to child workers is not only a matter of building a child-friendly environment within the school, but also promoting a broader, more political environment in which 'going to school' is part of the 'fundamental rights framework' for children. The geographical location of the action programme, supported by ILO-IPEC is in Kulkacherla Mandal, a very underdeveloped area with high concentration of girls working in the production of hybrid cotton seeds in cotton farms. Many of these girls are from the Lambadi tribes, known to be migratory in nature. Supported by an approach using social mobilization techniques, MFV established residential "bridge camps" to facilitate the transition of these farmer-child labourers into formal education, in a way, to help their social mobilisation through the process of their schooling more or less in a formal way.

MVF works towards these goals by building the capacities of the community in rural areas to promote formal school education and, on this basis, to eliminate child labour. Their efforts have been focused on the changing social norms, for example, allowing children to benefit from fundamental rights and development by going to school instead of going to work. At the village level, MVF works to create consensus within the communities on universal education and against child labour. The entire community is mobilized, through various techniques, including public rallies and theatre, to look at key issues, such as withdrawing girls from work and sending them to non-formal education bridge camps. Various village committees, representing elders, elected representatives, youth groups, teachers and parents are formed to take on a variety of functions, such as influencing the hiring practices of local employers, who hire girls; influencing the behaviour and attitude of parents and community members to send children to school and not to worksites; monitoring all aspects of the programme's implementation; reviewing children's performance in the school; and tracking children after bridge camps to ensure that they attend and remain in the school.

Depending on their age, children were withdrawn from work and placed in either short-term (six months) or long-term (18 to 24 months) residential bridge camps, which prepare them up to 7th grade. Using the MVF-developed Rapid Learning Technique and non-formal education curriculum, the camp courses aim ultimately at merging with the school curriculum, facilitating the mainstreaming of graduates to formal education. Camp teachers are selected from the local community and are trained in regular pedagogical subjects, such as languages, mathematics and science and also special subjects, such as child-sensitivity, adolescence and so on. As most of the girls, who attend the camps, come from the Lambadi tribes, who speak a different dialect than the language used in formal schools (Telugu), the camp teachers develop language skills of the children gradually through interaction and encouragement.

Minimal parallel structures were established alongside formal schools already available, using the existing government institutional infrastructures. In addition, when the State of Andhra Pradesh adopted the MVF's bridge camps model, the organization also provided considerable advice and support to ensure its effective implementation. Politicians from different parties in Kulkacherala Mandal joined together in establishing a forum to discuss strategies for removing children from bonded labour and cash crop farms (cotton seeds) in the area to move to school for their education and social mobilisation as the end product of their schooling.

An ILO-IPEC report revealed that there had been a considerable reduction in the incidence of child labour in the area following the MVF programme. It also successfully created consensus at the community level that school is the only alternative to prevent children from working as labour force and, through this consensus, succeeded in establishing social norms against child labour.

The MVF model has been replicated on a wider scale by the Andhra Pradesh government's Department of Social Welfare through its "Back to School Project", covering over 10,000 children each summer. MVF also plays a significant role in providing technical support to the state-led educational programmes.

An Exemplar: Out-of-School sisters Arti and Bharti show the way back to school.

As reported in *The Hindustan Times* on 18th July 2013, Aarti, 14 and her sister Bharti, 13, used to work in a shop, where they made nests. Unlike a few other children in the slums of Gurgaon Sector 12, where they lived, the two sisters had been to school till about the age of six.

"We had to discontinue their education as we weren't able to earn enough money in Gurgaon. We decided to shift to a village near Ghaziabad in Uttar Pradesh," said their mother Radha, who has been living in the slums with her family for the last 20 years.

The family—two daughters, a homemaker mother and a cobbler father—had moved out of Gurgaon for a brief period of six months in search for a better life, which led to the discontinuation of their studies.

"After returning, we never thought that we would be able to study. We didn't even hope to do so. So, we started helping out in the shop", said Aarti, who is now enrolled in Class 6 of a government school in Sector 14 with her younger sister Bharti.

Like in most cases, getting the duo admitted in a school was not easy. The volunteers of *Hindustan Times*' "You Read They Learn" initiative had to make several trips to the school to get these girls admitted.

"The school authorities said that Aarti had crossed the age for admission into primary section. But she did not know much to be admitted into the secondary school. Finally, they told us to shift her to middle school in Class 6, but she is studying the Class 4 syllabus," said Shivinder Narwal, student of YMCA, Faridabad and a 'YRTL' volunteer.

The other reason why the school created a fuss on admitting the two sisters was that they had studied in the same school earlier. But one fine day, they abruptly stopped attending the classes. So, the school asked them about it, if they would do it again. "But we promised them that no such thing would happen," recalled Narwal.

"I enjoy studying, but I never thought that it would be possible to study again. It is because of my sister and Shvinder bhaiyya that I am able to study once again," said Aarti.

Mid-day Meal Incentive

The mid-day meal scheme is a flagship programme of the Central Government. It is an incentive to children to attend the school studies. It has been a fairly successful scheme. There has been a debate on freshly made meal versus packed food. Packed food would surely be useful for remote areas where transportation is difficult, but the Court has asked the government to provide fresh food to children.

The scheme has been under criticism since 23 children died and dozens fell ill after eating the food served at Saran district in Bihar. A national level committee has been formed to look into several critical aspects of the scheme to prevent the recurrence of such incidents. The Committee of experts and representative of relevant ministries, like health, etc. have to look into critical aspects of the scheme, like hygiene, safety and nutrition in order to strengthen the scheme. There is also a need to have greater community mobilization and involvement of parents. This is primarily the responsibility of the School Management Committee. There is a need to monitor the scheme by the authorities and those responsible for its implementation.

2

Government Initiatives

Non-Formal Education

The non-formal education (NFE) scheme introduced in 1977-78 on a pilot basis and expanded in subsequent years, focused on out-of-school children in the 6-14 age group, who had remained outside the formal system due to socio-economic and cultural reasons. The scheme was initially limited to ten educationally backward states, covering urban slums, hilly, tribal and desert areas. As the scheme suffered from many lacunae—lack of enthusiasm among teachers, poor quality of training, ambiguity about curriculum and textbooks, lack of community participation, weak management system, insufficient outlay, lack of emphasis on mainstreaming etc.; and as most NFE centres were in habitations already served by formal schools, the programme was revised and renamed as *Education Guarantee Scheme and Alternative and Innovative Education* (EGS & AIE) in 2000. It provided for opening EGS schools in habitations, where there were no schools within a radius of one kilometre. The EGS&AIE scheme supported diversified strategies for out-of-school children including *bridge courses*, *back-to-school camps*, *seasonal hostels*, *summer camps*, *mobile teachers* and *remedial coaching*. The investment cost per child per year had also to be increased from Rs. 375 to Rs. 845 at the primary level centre and from Rs. 580 to Rs. 1,200 at the upper primary level over the years.

Residential and Non-Residential Bridge Courses

Under Sarva Shiksha Abhiyan programme, the Government of India provides educational support to nearly 20 crore children in about 14 lakh schools in the country with special focus on disadvantaged sections, such as SC/ST and minorities, particularly girls. During the implementation of SSA, to begin with direct mainstreaming and providing access to schooling could take care of the younger children (6-8 years). But the never-enrolled and drop-out children in the older age group (8-14 years) needed time for preparation to get mainstreamed in respective classes as per their age. The bridge courses provided facilities of accelerated learning through condensed courses to prepare them to get mainstreamed in regular schools. Short term (3-6 months) non-residential bridge courses (NRBCs) for children in the age group of 8-10 years, who needed shorter period for preparation to get mainstreamed in regular schools, remained in place. The objectives of the short-term courses aimed at habit formation accompanied by learning and practising basic language, mathematics and science skills. Short-term NRBCs are also run for older children (11 to 14 years), who had recently dropped out of school. As the drop-out and never-enrolled children in the age group of 11-14 years needed much more time for such preparation, so bridge courses of longer duration (9-18 months) are run for them.

Long-term NRBCs are also run for the 'difficult to reach' children (e.g. working children, children with special needs, children of sex workers) at a specified place throughout the year. Residential bridge courses (RBCs) are generally not run for short term. These are meant for children, who need extensive and intensive care to be prepared for mainstreaming. RBCs are for 'difficult-to-reach' children, never-enrolled children, drop-outs (mainly from the older age group) from scattered locations, child labour rescued from employers, or bonded child labour, wage earning or non-wage earning working children, who stay with their families, but bear the risk of dropping out even after enrolment in NRBCs or mainstreaming in formal schools. Accelerated learning facilities to acquire academic skills within the shortest possible time; condensed textbooks with lots of exercises; strong collaboration with regular schools; and regular monitoring and evaluations are some of the strategies adopted to run the bridge courses, so that these children are enabled to prepare themselves for mainstreaming as per their age group.

Other Alternative Schemes

Sometimes children, due to their adverse circumstances, face multiple obstacles in attaining even the bridge courses or fail to achieve the required skills within the short period for which these courses are run. The working children, children from nomadic communities, the child-domestic workers, never-enrolled children of very small habitations, children of construction workers, etc. sometimes are not in a position to join a regular school or even a bridge course during the day within the rigid time-schedule. Centre-based alternative facilities with longer duration and flexible timing and curriculum are run for these specific categories of children. The ultimate objective of running these centres is to mainstream the learners from these centres in regular schools in the long run.

Alternative Centres for Children in Madarsas and Maktabs

A small proportion of Muslim children are enrolled in *Madarsas* and *Maktabs*. Many of these children do not attend a regular school. While the effort under SSA has been to mainstream these children in regular schools, it was a felt necessity that the general education component of Madarsas/Maktabs could be strengthened wherever these institutions are willing to do so. Such Madarsas/Maktabs receive assistance under SSA for funding extra teachers, teacher training, textbooks, etc. for the teaching of general subjects.

Establishing and Running Human Development Centres (HDCs)

- Hard-to-reach children, children of specific communities with specific socio-economic characteristics are identified through the mandatory annual survey by the State, as also through qualitative feedback from the cluster and block level personnel.

- On the basis of objective evaluation of collected data and feedback, the District or the State Project Office of SSA decide the most suitable plan to address the educational needs of these children. The priority here is not immediate mainstreaming or bridging, but bringing them under the fold of education.
- Justification for starting such flexible centres needs to be strongly backed by qualitative data. When assured about the same, the district and state authorities design the structure of the centre, curriculum, and most importantly, the extra-curricular activities. It is important to motivate and lure the otherwise uninterested children and parents. The temporary nature of these centres is pre-integrated in this design for implementation.
- In many instances, the responsibilities of running these centres are given to the Non-Governmental Organisations (NGOs). The State SSA programme invites applications from NGOs, providing details of children, communities and geographical locations. Specific NGOs are selected for specific groups of children on the basis of expertise and other criteria.
- The Education Volunteers (EVs) are provided training on motivational skills, extra-curricular activities and teaching-learning processes. They are required to maintain a regular and close contact with the families and children, so as to ensure their attendance and participation in activities, thereby, enhancing the possibility of their mainstreaming in the near future.
- The focus in HDC is to develop a habit amongst children to come to the education centre, extend facilities to learn the basics of language and mathematics to develop their latent talents and to motivate children for continuing their education.

Select Case Studies

***Continuing Education of Migrating Children* (A Joint Initiative by SSA Andhra Pradesh, SSA Orissa and Action Aid India)**

SSA Andhra Pradesh, SSA Orissa and Action Aid India made a joint survey in the year 2004 to address the educational needs of the Brick Kiln migrating children of selected blocks of three districts—Rangareddy, Medak and Nalgonda of Andhra Pradesh. Block level SSA officials, school teachers of the concerned villages and volunteers from SSA Orissa participated in the survey to chalk out the Action plan and identify places to set up non-residential and residential bridge courses (NRBCs & RBCs) for these children. The identification of a total of 2721 children in the age group of 6-14 years and 1535 children in the age group of 0-5 years in six blocks of three districts led to the setting up of Early Childhood Care Centres for children of 3-5 years of age, non-residential bridge courses for children of 6-9 years of age and residential bridge courses for children in the age group of 9-14 years. SSA Andhra Pradesh instructed its district officials to provide mid-day meal and learning material to the children of NRBCs and RBCs. By the first week of January 2005, NRBCs were opened at the identified places. By the end of 2005-06, the initiative was successful in enrolling 2721 children in the RBCs & NRBCs; 1943 of these children joined back their original schools; and 1306 were promoted to the next standard. Presently, the initiative is covering only six selected blocks of Andhra Pradesh. The extent of migration to brick-kilns and other industries being a large one, a larger coverage is needed to ensure the continuation of education of all children, who seasonally migrate to other states and districts.

Bhonga Shala (for Brick-Kiln Children in Thane District of Maharashtra)

Bhonga Shala is an innovation to provide education to children from brick-kilns in Thane district of Maharashtra. In Marathi, '*Bhonga*' means a temporary hut and '*Shala*' a school. So, *Bhonga Shala* is a 'school run in a temporary hut'. It was estimated that 25000 children migrate to the brick-kilns of Thane district of Maharashtra every year. Most of them work in these brick-kilns and some of the wards just accompany their parents. Maharashtra is the second most urbanised state in India and most of its 42 districts have hundreds of brick-kilns. Unfortunately, no estimate is available on how many children in Maharashtra lose at least six months of education due to migration to brick-kilns. However, in Thane, the migrating population is predominantly tribal—the Warlis, Katkaris, Mahadeo Kolis, Malhar Kolis, Thakurs and Kokanas.

Among these six tribes, the Katkaris are the most backward, socio-economically and educationally. The literacy rate amongst them is a mere nine per cent and female literacy is hardly one per cent. Children accompanying their migrating parents are compelled to work to supplement the family income. They are not counted separately and are taken as part of the family's income because the payments made here are based on the number of bricks produced. The children are engaged in various activities like sieving the coal dust, preparing the dough for bricks and carrying as many as 10 to 12 bricks at a time. They work for 10-14 hours a day. The coal dust affects their skin, hair, eyes and lungs. To clean the mud, they have to stand in thigh deep dirty water.

Vidhayak Sansad, a local NGO, started five *Bhonga Shalas* in 1995 in two blocks of Thane district. Starting and running a *Bhonga Shalas* is much more than opening an education centre in the month of December and closing it in April. The process begins with the recruitment and selection of teachers and is followed by conducting surveys of children in brick kilns. The sites for *Bhonga Shala* are decided according to the number of children available. The construction of the schools begins after informing the brick kiln owners and requesting their cooperation. Enrolment of children and meetings with parents go hand in hand. The actual teaching-learning process begins after the enrolment. During the survey, it was found that many children have never been to school; most of them, who ever attended a school, do not remember what they learnt earlier in their schools. Preliminary tests are conducted to find out their actual abilities in order to accordingly admit them in the respective standard or class.

Sakhar Shala *(for Sugar-Cane labour children in Maharashtra)*

Sakhar Shalas are temporary schools in the settlements of sugar-cane cutters, which intend to provide primary education to children of sugar-cane labourers. The aim of the *Sakhar Shala* intervention is to help children continue their education, which is severely hampered due to migration. It also helps children to get back to mainstream education.

Janarth, an Aurangabad-based NGO in Maharashtra, started this innovative intervention of *Sakhar Shalas* in the year 2001-02 with 882 children of migrant labourers at two cooperative sugar factories in Ahmednagar district. Today, the organisation runs *Sakhar Shalas* in five districts of the state—Ahmednagar, Pune, Nasik, Sangli and Satara. Presently, there are 73 such temporary schools catering to 4256 migrating children.

The ultimate objective of *Sakhar Shala* is to improve the quality of life of the migrant labourers by providing quality education to their children. The model focuses on: (i) acquisition of basic reading, writing and numeric skills; (ii) imbibing a sound value system; (iii) physical fitness; and (iv) preparing for higher education. The *Sakhar Shalas* concentrate on competency-based teaching for the young children to enhance their capacities and potentials and to help them have greater control over their lives. At the primary level, the competencies are defined for three subjects—language, mathematics and science. Apart from developing these competencies, the teaching-learning process in *Sakhar Shalas* emphasises on using scientific equipments and apparatus, using remedial methods and making education an enjoyable and interesting experience for children. It lends hand in making children keen observers and able thinkers. *Sakhar Shalas* also aim at incorporating value system in the students so as to help them become good citizens. Values imparted include nationalism, integration, gender equality, respect for physical labour, scientific temper, punctuality and cleanliness.

Vindam Radio Programme *(for Out-of-School children at Chaduvukundam in Andhra Pradesh)*

The programme, conceived by SSA Andhra Pradesh to prepare the out-of-school children before mainstreaming or enrolling in alternative initiatives like bridge courses, covering working children, children involved in household work, never-enrolled ones and long duration drop-outs. Traditionally, Andhra Pradesh had a large number of such out-of-school children. School was an almost alien place for them. Education not being a priority, they seldom got opportunities to enjoy their childhood, let alone their school. Even after enrolment, if any, these children tended to drop out very soon. So, it was deemed important that these children are pre-prepared or readied first, before putting them even in bridge courses.

Vindam Chaduvukundam was planned after holding a series of consultations between SSA officials, All India Radio (AIR), DIET personnel and other academicians. The content and structure of the radio programme was designed by SSA Andhra Pradesh while recording, anchoring, songs, music and broadcasting was taken care of by the AIR. By the end of March 2006, a total of 6321 centres covered 109274 out-of-school children through this radio programme. Besides these 6321 exclusive centres, 844 Residential Bridge

Courses, 94 Kasturba Gandhi Balika Vidyalayas and 1199 Non-Residential Bridge Courses also made arrangements for children to listen to the radio programme as per the schedule.

Tent Schools *(at work-sites for labour migrants in Karnataka)*

Seasonal migration of children, with or without families, has added a large chunk to the already existing out-of-school children, many of them being never-enrolled and some being drop-outs. According to estimates, nearly two-three crore people seasonally migrate every year. The duration of these migrations depends on the nature of job in which they are engaged. Long term migration for six-eight months happens for those engaged in sugar-cane cultivation, crushing sites and working in brick-kilns, salt-pans, charcoal and construction industries. Agricultural activities like paddy cultivation attract short duration migration. Karnataka has high intrastate and interstate migration.

`The State SSA authorities realised that it was easier to provide NRBCs at work-sites and for mainstreaming rather than running residential bridge courses (RBCs). Low cost temporary education centres called Tent Schools, built at work-sites, mainly construction sites, mines and sugar-cane fields, provided bridging facilities to the migrating children. In 2005-06, a total of 216 tent schools were opened and 6699 learners were enrolled. Of these, 140 were opened just in five districts—Gulbarga, Bangalore (urban), Bellary, Mysore and Dharwad, primarily engaged in stone quarry, iron-ore mining, building and road construction that attracted the major inward labour migration.

School-on-Boat *(for 'Donelu' fishing population in Andhra Pradesh*

School-on-Boat is not a school. It is only a beginning to the process of ensuring education for children, who live in boats on the 'sea approaching canal' at Uppalanka Mondi of Karapa Mandal, East Godavari District. Nearly 70 years back, a group of fishermen (exact number not known) from fishing islands—Balusu Tippo, Yetimoga, Palasa, etc., migrated to Uppalanka Mondi, hoping to catch fish in the sea and earn a livelihood. They migrated from their native places due to high tide condition of the sea there that had made fishing highly costly for these very poor fishermen community.

But the local fishermen community denied these migrating families any right to live either on the main land or do fishing in the sea. They were permitted only to stay on their respective boats (*Donelu*) and do fishing in the four km long canal leading to the sea. Life being so hard back home, the migrating families had to agree, despite difficult conditions. They continued with their demand to live on the mainland, which stands denied even till date. Over the years, they married mostly within the '*Donelu*' families. A new married family started its own '*Donelu*' and the number gradually has grown to 180. Ironically, they get no fish in the canal now and survive only by collecting snails. Education seemed remote in such circumstances.

The process of educating children from '*Donelus*', however, starts with (i) motivating them through 'School on Boat'; (ii) further motivation and bridging at short-term NRBC on the bank of sea approaching canal; (iii) bridging at nearby RBC Camp; (iv) formal school education at Day/Residential Formal School; and leading to (v) meaningful vocational training.

After three months of orientation, a group of 'readied' children were enrolled in a nearby Residential Bridge Course and that too only when the children themselves and their parents were ready for it. Books, notebooks, clothes and other facilities were provided to facilitate these children. The EVs at the residential Bridge Course centres were also duly oriented about these children, the difficulties they were facing, with a caution not to segregate them from others. These children were allowed to visit their '*Donelus*' more frequently in the initial months and their parents also visited the RBCs as and when they wished.

This has created a sense of belongingness and has given confidence to the parents, who were otherwise, naturally, not enthusiastic about education of their children. After successfully completing their courses at RBC, these children were enrolled in regular schools; and all girls were sent to the nearby APRPRP residential high school at Chollangipeta.

Right to Education Act

A Century Old Dream Becomes Alive

The 'Right of Children to Free and Compulsory Education (RTE) Act 2009 marks a landmark historical moment for the nation's children. It took almost hundred years to come since Gopal Krishna Gokhale unsuccessfully tried for such an Act in 1911. For the first time in India's history, children are guaranteed their right to quality education by the state, making the family and community alive and responsible for their wards' school education. Only a few countries in the world have such a national provision to ensure child-centred, child-friendly education to help all children develop to their fullest potential. An estimated eight million, six to fourteen year olds in India were out-of-school children in 2009. The Right to Education Act 2009 is a move ahead in the direction of 100 per cent literacy in India. It has put forward provisions to make the concept of enrolment and retention of all students at least up to 8th class successful. A promotional step in this direction is 'Age-Appropriate Enrolment' drive to facilitate RTE implementation.

Problems in Implementation

The Right of Children to Free and Compulsory Education Act 2009 came into force on 1 April 2010. The Government is committed to ensure elementary education for all children aged 6-14 through its flagship programme, the "Sarva Shiksha Abhiyan" (2001). Though efforts to provide free and compulsory education are being made, in reality, these are not accessible everywhere due to a large number of issues and the multiplicity of challenges in its implementation at the grassroot level.

The exploration of possible solutions and improvement in the strategies for its successful implementation are being made at various levels. Yet, the gap appears glaring and defying. The gap between the present school system and the provisions of RTE is a major challenge in the implementation of the RTE. There are issues related to formal schooling upto elementary stage, especially, in unaided/ private schools. Equity, accessibility, retention and success with quality are being addressed as the main concerns of elementary education under the Sarva Shiksha Abhiyan.

The focus of RTE is primarily on ten concerns as follows:

1. Pupil teacher ratio (PTR)
2. Age-appropriate enrolment
3. Infrastructural facilities
4. Existing curriculum
5. Inclusive setting
6. Readiness for innovative pedagogic practices
7. CCE—a vital requirement of RTE
8. School Management Committees (SMCs)

9. Role of community participation
10. Change of attitude of the stakeholders and their commitment for making 'Education for All Children' a reality, with the support of the RTE law.

Age-Appropriate Enrolment

Section 4 of RTE Act (2009) highlights special concern for children not admitted or who have not completed elementary education. "Where a child above six years of age has not been admitted in any school, or though admitted, could not complete his or her elementary education, then, he or she shall be admitted in a class appropriate to his or her age;

Provided that where a child is directly admitted in a class appropriate to his or her age, then, he or she shall, in order to be at par with others, have a right to receive special training, in such manner, and within such time limit as may be prescribed; Provided further that a child so admitted to elementary education shall be entitled to free education until completion of elementary education after fourteen years."

According to the provision of 'Age-Appropriate' as stated in the Right to Education Act 2009, different age group children have to be admitted in the classes corresponding to their respective age as follows:

Class	*Age-Group*
For Class I	- 5 to 6 yrs
Class II	- 6 to 7 yrs
Class III	- 7 to 8 yrs
Class IV	- 8 to 9 yrs
Class V	- 9 to 10 yrs
Class VI	- 10-11 yrs
Class VII	- 11-12 yrs
Class VIII	- 12-13 yrs

Problem Areas-in-Specific

There are general classroom problems, which create difficulties for teachers and students in the implementation of the concept of age appropriate enrolment and further in mainstreaming the out-of-school children.

The problems faced by teachers include the following:

- Teaching Problem—Pedagogic difficulties to teach children, who do not even know the sounds of basic alphabets.
- Individual Attention—How to deal with individualized problems of so many students of different learning capacities in overcrowded classes (as is the current reality of the classroom size)?
- Classroom Academic Integration—How to integrate such students, who have gap in their studies, with regular students?
- Mid-day Meal—Teachers also have to take care of the menu of mid-day meal, check quality and maintain its records; it thus becomes difficult to maintain or manage the classes properly even at the primary stage.
- Attendance of Students—Students find it unattractive, sitting for the day only in a combined class, other classes being useless to them. They bunk the classes, creating a lot of problems for teachers as regards students' absence from class and their further learning.

Problems Faced by Students: Following are some of the other problem areas, which students encounter in the classroom.

- Inferiority complex—Students with low academic achievement feel inferior while studying with their class fellows having higher achievement.
- Teasing—Those students, who have never attended school before, are teased by regularly attending students, which causes a social acceptance challenge for such student by other fellow mates, which, in turn, is not easy.
- Feeling of discomfort by the students taking extra classes with younger students.
- Lack of academic orientation—Out-of-school children generally lack academic interest and orientation. As a result,

academic achievement of these children is low. Due to their social maladjustment, there remains the problem of academic integration of these children with the mainstream, which becomes yet more serious.

- Diverse social background of children, their differential learning levels, learning gaps between home and age-appropriate class create the problem of learning the school subjects, specially language and mathematics in lower classes.

3

Inclusive Education and Mainstreaming

"Children, who learn together, learn to live together."
(UNESCO: Delors Commission, 1996)

Inclusive education is an approach and philosophy that provides all students with community membership and greater opportunities for academic and social achievement. It is about making sure that each and every student feels welcome and that their unique needs and learning styles are attended to and valued. Inclusive education is seen as "a process of addressing and responding to the diversity of needs of all learners through increasing participation in learning, cultures and communities, and reducing exclusion from education and from within education" (UNESCO, 1996). Within an inclusive education approach, the goal is to ensure that learning environments are fostered where individual needs are met and every student has an opportunity to succeed, in that the whole education system facilitates learning environments, where teachers and learners embrace and welcome the challenges and benefits of diversity.

Inclusive Education: Government Legislation and Constitutional Provisions

The Constitution of India does not explicitly include children with disabilities in the provisions made for education, though its Article 41 does mention people with disabilities. It says, "The State shall, within the limits of its economic development, make effective provisions for securing the right to work, to education and to public assistance in cases of unemployment, old age, sickness, disablement and in other cases of undesired want." It does not mandate free and compulsory education as a fundamental right and is merely a directive principle to guide the state policy. Article 45, however, does state that free and compulsory education should be provided for ALL children until they complete the age of 14 though the term, 'ALL' has never been specifically explained.

In December 1995, the Government of India had a bill passed in the Parliament called "The Equal Opportunities, Protection of Rights and Full Participation Bill for Persons with Disability", the Disability Act 1995. In short, that specifically mandates (Chapter V on Education) that every child with disability should have access to free and adequate education.

The 93rd amendment to the Indian Constitution, passed in December 2001, affirmed the Government's commitment to Education for All (EFA), known as Sarva Shiksha Abhiyan (SSA). Its preamble explicitly states that this includes children with disabilities. This policy aims at all children in the 6 to 14 age group being able to complete eight years of schooling by the year 2010. The SSA gives importance to early childhood care and education and appropriate intervention for children with special needs also and makes special reference to the education of the girl child. The positive factor is the change incorporated in the Education Act by adding a pertinent clause, which clarifies that the term "ALL" includes children with disabilities too. This led to the concept of Inclusive Education at the primary and secondary school levels.

The Draft National Policy for Persons with Disability circulated on 15th of June 2005 invited comments from stakeholders. With specific reference to education and in recognition of the fact that one model may not be suitable to a country with such a diverse population and the wide diversity of needs for persons with disability in different environmental and social conditions, the policy covers a variety of educational options, such as special education, distance education, itinerant teacher model, remedial teaching, home-based CBR model, home-based education, education through an open learning system, alternative schooling among others. Many specialized and national as well as state level institutions have been established from time to time to advise and assist the Ministry. For instance, the one, pertinent to intellectual disability, the National Institute for Mental Handicap, came in existence far back in 1984.

Other Initiatives

The Right to Education Act 2009 being implemented since April 1, 2010, gives legal right to every child between 6 to 11 years for free and compulsory primary education.

Certain other major initiatives, undertaken by the Central/State governments, also have had their causal influence and impact on classroom practices with an inclusive setting. Some of these are:

Implementation of the RTE Act

The implementation of the RTE Act envisages greater and wider heterogeneity in learners' socio-economic background and cognitive abilities, especially, differently abled children of mild nature. Schools with inclusive setting need to think of meeting the problems of changing composition of the classroom today. Recently, the Hon'ble Supreme Court of India directed all private and public schools to admit 25 per cent students of the economically weaker sections of the society. This, too, would result in economically and socially heterogeneous inclusive classrooms.

No Detention Policy

Recently, the government announced 'no detention policy' upto class 8th and introduced Continuous and Comprehensive Evaluation (CCE) in schools. CBSE has prepared a detailed scheme, which is now being implemented in all its affiliated schools in the country. The impact of this move is likely to be available in due course of time.

CBSE Examination Optional at Secondary Stage

Due to academic stress on secondary school students, the CBSE has made its examination at the end of grade X optional for the students; they may or may not appear at this examination and depend upon the school-based continous and comprehensive evaluation

(CCE) of their achievement. Practically, it has become optional for the school and not so for individual students. Admission to +2 level would be made on the basis of CCE/Board results.

Diverse Class Composition

In the context of recent developments in the field of school education, the nature of classroom composition is increasingly changing. The primary classes have wide heterogeneity in terms of students' level of intelligence (in multiple senses), social diversity, economic imbalance (double disadvantaged learners), diverse interest and purpose of education. In this context, the present pedagogic principles may not work effectively. The innovative pedagogy for the poor/disadvantaged needs to be worked out and tried at the earliest. The role of teachers and teacher educators is, consequently, getting very significant.

ICT Intervention

In order that teaching at the primary level is progressively realized, innovative pedagogy involving ICT intervention shall have to be experimented and tried out for enhancing the pupils' learning. Incentive and encouragement through in-service training programmes have also to be provided at the earliest to help the teachers to use the ICT effectively at the primary level of school education.

Mainstreaming

It is very important to mainstream not only the disadvantaged children, who come from urban slums, rural farm labour specially in hilly, coastal, desert and tribal areas of the country, but also those, who have never gone to school or are school drop-outs. Since they have to get admission in age-appropriate school classes, this poses a big challenge in the implementation of the RTE Act 2009 as well as an immediate concern for their mainstreaming.

Imminent Concerns

The education system in India has to be compromised at many levels to meet the major concerns before mainstreaming, which could be viewed as follows, along various parameters:

Inclusion vs Mainstreaming: Inclusion and mainstreaming are different terms. Proponents of mainstreaming hold that students with special needs be placed solely in the general education setting, when they can meet traditional academic expectations with minimal assistance. Yet, simply placing students with special needs in the regular classroom is not enough to impact learning. Teachers in inclusive schools are asked to vary their teaching styles to meet the diverse learning styles of a diverse population of students. Only then can the individual needs of all our students be met. Schools of the future need to ensure that each student receives individual attention, accommodation and support that will result in meaningful learning. It involves a set of sub-concerns, too, such as:

- We no longer see the child as a priority. We have become very conscious of the need to educate our children. But there is hardly any academic motivation to generate this interest; rather there is only economic motivation.
- Education is largely seen as a route to white-collar jobs. This is due to the present education system, which has moulded generations only to think that all worth is measured in terms of money. Inclusive education in India is no exception. It needs to contend simply with the whims of the present system of education provided under the Integrated Education pattern.
- Varying statistics are available on the prevalence of intellectual disabilities. Surveys conducted by the National Sample Survey Organisation (NSSO) in 2002 and the national Census in 2001 show varying figures—the NSSO quoting 1.8 per cent (1.85 crore of the country's population) and the Census quoting 2.19 per cent of the population (2.19 crore).
- Need for parental involvement.

- Need to develop students' sense of belonging to the school/ community.
- Promoting school culture and environment that are child-friendly as well as conducive to effective learning.
- Need for holistic approach based on inclusive education that can be adapted to the complexities and specificities of national situations.
- Need to strengthen teachers' competencies/skills for inclusive education.

Challenges

> "The illiterate of the 21st century will not be those, who cannot read and write, but those who cannot learn, unlearn, and relearn." (UNESCO, 1996)

The challenges being enormous, only some of them are stated here as examples:

- Designing curriculum to include all students and ensure equal access to all levels of education and all types of schools (including access, processes and results);
- Alleviating the status of students with special educational needs: from a clinical approach to a rights-based approach;
- Obviating inequality and discrimination among students based on socio-economic, ethnic and cultural profiles (e.g., the competencies and learning outcomes achieved);
- Increased opportunities to learn and share best practices, research and pilot projects; and
- Supporting the strategic role of tertiary education in the training of teachers in inclusive education practices.

Special Training for Out-of-School Children

Special training for the never-enrolled children or those, who dropped out before completing the elementary education would require identification of children, who must be enrolled. For this, the State Government, Local Authority and School Management

Committee will need to undertake a community level school mapping exercise. The neighbourhood and school mapping exercise will have to be followed by: (i) immediate enrolment in the school; (ii) organisation of special training of flexible duration to enable the child to be at par with other children; (iii) actual admission of the child in the age-appropriate class on completion of special training, and his/her participation in all class activities; and (iv) continued support to the child, once admitted to the regular school, so that the child can integrate with the class socially, emotionally and academically.

The duration of special training may be flexible, varying from three months to two years, depending on the child's needs. Special training may be in the form of residential or non-residential courses organised, preferably in the premises of the school, but if such facilities are not available in school, alternate facilities, which are safe, secure and accessible, may be identified and used. At the end of the duration of special training for a particular child, the suitability of placing the child in a class may be reviewed. For example, if a ten year old child was admitted to Class IV, and has received two years of special training till the age of 12, an assessment may be made as to whether the child could cope better in Class V or VI in the formal school, and the child would be appropriately placed. Even after a child is appropriately placed in the formal school, he/she may continue to receive special attention by the teacher to successfully integrate with the rest of the class academically and emotionally.

4

Education for Integration

With the enactment of the Right to Education Act 2009 and other Government initiatives, there has been a significant expansion in the number of students participating in elementary education particularly, from the under-represented, lower socio-economic and disadvantaged groups of children with wide-ranging levels of preparedness needing different types of pedagogy. It is important to underline that enrolment figures alone understate the extent of deficit in providing basic education of good quality; that mere enrolment for education is insufficient; and that students need to be able to succeed, too. Ensuring access to education is a precondition for full realization of the right to education. Without access, it is not possible to guarantee the right to education, let alone the quality of education.

Providing access to schools secures only one part of the right to education. Success may mean different things for different students, but definitely, it ought to include the retention of students and successful completion of their education. Thus, the goal of universalisation is not only related to universal access and retention, but also to achievement of the identified competencies by all children. The issue of drop-outs and their integration in school requires immediate action; it is a serious phenomenon that deserves priority by all involved in education: government, planners, decision-makers, community, family and teachers.

Retaining themselves in school is a challenge for many children. For some students, dropping out is the culmination of the years of academic struggle due to dual pressures of family and school life simultaneously; as well as social maladjustment with peers and teachers; and sometimes being bored and seeing no connection between school and "real" life. Each student's performance is influenced both by school and non-school factors. Both morally and educationally, institutions have a duty to do everything that they can to help students achieve success in their education. Valuing education in life is very important, particularly, when it comes to our most vulnerable and disadvantaged children struggling for attention within the school system. High rates of withdrawal and low rates of satisfaction may have reputational, economic, ethical and legal implications for schools and governments, besides personal and financial disadvantages for individuals. Just passing the RTE Act 2009 would not suffice; proper intention, attention and actions are required for making children retain themselves in schools and learn something productive. A fair and inclusive system that makes the advantages of education available to all is one of the most powerful forces to make society more equitable. There may be increased enrolment, but many students' learning remains inadequate, which needs to be taken care of immediately in an inclusive and integral way.

Integration

Concept and Nature

Education needs to be understood in the context of availability, accessibility, acceptability and adaptability. Availability examines whether education is generally available; accessibility focuses on various obstacles in accessing education; acceptability evaluates various aspects of the content of education; and adaptability implies whether education is adapted to the needs of various categories of learners. Integration may mean different things to different people, nonetheless, definite emphasis remains on the retention of the students in the sector for successful completion of the courses within the specified time-period. This may be achieved only when education is adaptable. Integrated education recognises every child's entitlement to gain full access to a broad and balanced curriculum, alongside or together with their peers in a mainstream setting in the local community, wherever possible, enabling full and active participation in all activities of the school to gain the highest possible level of achievement. The education system should necessarily have the goal of enabling every student to perform to the best of their abilities and help lessen the potentially adverse effects of students' background characteristics on their educational performance.

Interventions and approaches to improve students' retention and success should essentially strive for mainstreaming of all students to ensure their participation to their benefit. Education for Integration means developing a continuum of provisions matching the continuum of learners' needs, so that no child, whatever be the circumstance, remains disadvantaged from the benefits of education. This is to be achieved by the retention of all students and ensuring maximum success to them all by removing barriers that stand against their achievement. Particular attention should be paid to students, who tend to opt out or fail to engage, and provide additional support to the learners, if necessary. Such efforts would lead to integration and help mainstreaming with due success.

Dimensions of Integration

Integration has several dimensions like physical, social, emotional and academic, as briefly discussed here.

Physical Integration

Physical integration implies the availability and provision of access to physical facilities to everyone. Universal access to schooling facilities either within the habitation or at a reasonable walking distance is one of the important pre-requisites for integration. Reducing the distance to schools could help boost educational access for students. However, this may not be a sufficient condition, as the existence or the availability of educational facility may not imply for sure that it would be available to be used by all or is usable to optimal efficiency. It does imply the availability of proper infrastructure, adequate number of teachers (as per norm), prescribed usable space per child, textbooks for all children, drinking water facilities and toilets, a small library with access to books, meant for children, for all the students, exercise books, enough stationery for every child, etc. provided by the state, school, community, etc.

Social Integration

Social integration means the extent to which students feel that they 'fit in', particularly in the school environ in a social sense. Social integration would entail those experiences that help connect learners to the educational environment that aid in their psycho-social development; and that contribute to their overall satisfaction in the schools. Migration and mobility may be important challenges for social cohesion and there may also be longstanding issues of integrating minorities, different castes, etc. Fair, wholesome and inclusive education is the key to these challenges. Equity in education enhances social cohesion and trust. Curriculum issues, such as treating learning as an academic and social milieu; the curriculum adapted according to the needs of the learners; and choosing curricular structures that increase the chances of students' success do help enhance social integration.

Emotional Integration

Emotional integration would help the struggling students sustain themselves within the system. Children, who may be victims of violence, need special protection and care. So also those bullied by peers or threatened by teachers or parents; they need special care. Emotional disadvantage is more likely to be experienced by students from low socio-economic background, students from rural and remote locations, and students with disabilities, learning difficulties or other special needs as their peers may not readily try to adjust with them. Schools ought to help such students overcome such barriers for their integration in the mainstream.

Academic Integration

Some students may not be able to understand what is being taught in the classroom; maybe, due to missing their earlier classes or may not comprehend what is happening in the class because of lack of previous knowledge. This could certainly be the cause of their academic under-achievement. Academic integration means raising the achievement of all learners, respecting and celebrating their diversity and promoting their optimum education. Also, motivating the school environment to tally with the nature and behaviour of children, so that they could enjoy learning. Disadvantaged students may need better than average experiences to be able to perform better and overcome their difficulties. Academic integration would entail that all students have equal opportunity to realise their educational potential—irrespective of their individual, economic or social circumstances, or their level of ability. The provision of appropriate learning opportunities for disadvantaged students would require some specific pedagogical and classroom management practices. For instance, schools may have to play a role in compensating for the lack of support and encouragement that they might not receive from home. The focus has to be on the development of the most effective possible means of enabling children to access the mainstream curriculum in the schools to boost their achievement.

Integration Strategies

The basic strategy behind integration is to design and provide suitable supports—innovative approaches to learning, differentiated instruction, curricular adaptations etc.,—for every student in the classroom. Covering the entire spectrum of learners, it would ensure better achievement and well-being of the most vulnerable children, also including the out-of-school children admitted in school. Some of the viable strategies may be like the following:

- Place children, not institutions, at the centre of educational endeavour.
- One way of improving performance and preventing drop-out is to identify at-risk students early and take remedial actions quickly. This may involve monitoring information on attendance, performance and involvement in school activities. Have a concrete plan to improve outcomes and prevent drop-out.

- Services of support staff like counsellors, nurses, liaison officers, special educators, etc. should be availed to help school personnel develop in these areas. Create a congenial environment that may help disadvantaged children remain at school.
- An encouraging school system like school health programme would promote good health and healthy habits among children. Various activities could be planned and implemented to make the school environs attractive for the students to help them remain stay put in the school and participate in all the school programmes.
- Schools must address different difficulties faced by students—emotional, behavioural and learning difficulties. The counsellors in school should help the at-risk students.
- Schools must take a whole school approach to help students stay in school, where classroom practices, co-curricular activities and the informal curriculum should be brought together to build up the students holistically. Curriculum transaction has to take into account the distinctiveness of the child, child's personality, intelligence and potentials, to nurture every child in all dimensions of development—spiritual, moral, cognitive, emotional, imaginative, aesthetic, social and physical.
- Develop staff skills and confidence. Identify the cases and be proactive in retaining the at-risk students. Inculcate capacity to respond to students' individual needs; recognise the causes of their underachievement and adopt remedial mechanisms. Encourage high aspirations for all students, regardless of their background. For this, provide for regular in-service training programmes for teachers and heads of schools.
- Besides classroom intervention, involve parents, seeking their support for their children's learning. Children and their parents should be informed and convinced about benefits of education in terms of economic, social and emotional gains.
- Monetary and nutritional incentives (like scholarships, mid-day meal) may be implemented so as to cover the

opportunity cost of attending the school. Merit scholarships should be encouraged to motivate children to put in extra effort.

- More flexible approaches to formal schooling can respond to the needs of many children, who are out-of-school/have dropped out so that they may be inducted back in schools. The strategies like double shift schools, evening schools, Non-Formal Education Centres and Alternative Schools can also be planned for overcoming constraints in access to education.

Teachers' Role

Teachers play a central role in the integration of vulnerable students in the mainstream. Some of the tasks that a teacher may do for the integration of out-of-school children in the mainstream of school education include:

- Peers be taught to respect and support the students with disabilities, so also socially disadvantaged students. The system of reward and punishment be discarded to help retain all children in school.
- Acquire the skills to meet the learning needs of disadvantaged students.
- Use fun and games in promoting learning. Introduce the play-way method to bring the out-of-school children back to the school. Prescribe this method in the curriculum.
- Evaluation as a mechanism would enhance students' self-worth, to better their performance rather than classifying them as pass or fail. Use of formative assessment should be made for strengthening the learning of students.
- Use teaching strategies that are responsive to the learning strengths and needs of students from diverse linguistic, cultural, religious and socio-economic backgrounds. Engage them through a richer menu of academic and alternative co-curricular activities (CCA).
- Provide remedial and/or compensatory education to students, who fall behind. Remedial education should be

according to the needs of the students and not like a capsule meant for all the weak students in the class. Customised Lessons and Support Groups should be planned to preview upcoming lessons and fill in the knowledge gaps. Elective extra-help courses, tightly linked to core curriculum, should be organised for such students.

- Engage parents and the community to give initiatives and innovative ideas to help better the schooling of their wards.
- Foster a culture in the class to respect diversity in the student population rather than expecting or promoting similar behaviour in all types of students.
- Relate class activities with their life experiences to make them feel the utility of the educational endeavour they are engaged in. Develop self-esteem and confidence among students and an ability to apply knowledge and skills in diverse circumstances and purposes to make their learning relevant.
- Invite views of children and give them due weightage so that they feel important.
- Develop an environment to help build positive relationship between teachers and students. Every school child should be made to believe that there is an adult they can turn to when they face a difficult issue, even if it be a personal one.
- Ensure quality basic education for all, with an emphasis on gender equality, eliminating disparities of all kinds. School should also offer children a safe and secure environment, with support, supervision and socialization.

5

Early Pedagogical Interventions and Exciting Activities

Over the years, there has been a significant spatial and numerical expansion of elementary schools in the country. Access and enrolment at the primary stage of education have reached near universal levels. The number of out-of-school children has reduced significantly. The gender gap in elementary education has narrowed and the percentage of children belonging to scheduled castes and tribes enrolled in the schools is nearly proportionate to their population. Yet, the goal of universal elementary education continues to elude. There remains an unfinished agenda of universal education at the upper primary stage. The number of children, particularly children from disadvantaged groups and weaker sections, who dropped out of school before completing upper primary education, still remains high. The quality of learning achievement is not always entirely satisfactory even in the case of children, who complete elementary education. We are still unable to retain children in schools. It is proved through the high drop-out rates and low attendance have also become major challenges in achieving the UEE goals. Such situation calls for reviewing the school improvement initiatives and working out strategies for strengthening them.

Elementary education in the country has now been given high priority both by the Central and the State governments. The number of interventions have been made to ensure total participation of children as well as quality education for all. Access to school has expanded with investment on: (i) physical infrastructure, school building, functional toilets, availability of safe drinking water, child-friendly classrooms, etc.; and (ii) human resources, like appointing teachers, non-teaching staff and other functionaries, besides local level contribution of school management committees (SMCs), parents, community members, etc. in the day-to-day functioning of the school. Free and compulsory elementary education is now a Constitutional Fundamental Right according to the Right to Education Act 2009 that too aims at achieving the government's goal of universal elementary education. Sarva Shikha Abhiyan (SSA) forms the government's flagship platform to achieve that aim. The majority of our schools are covered under SSA.

Special Provisions for Out-of-School Children

There is a special provision for children not admitted or who have not completed elementary education under Section 4 of RTE Act 2009 that says, "Where a child above six years of age has not been admitted in any school or though admitted, could not complete his or her elementary education, then, he or she shall be admitted in a class appropriate to his or her age:

Provided that where a child is directly admitted in a class appropriate to his or her age, then, he or she shall, in order to be at par with others, have a right to receive special training, in such manner, and within such time-limit as may be prescribed.

Provided further that a child so admitted to elementary education shall be entitled to free education until the completion of elementary education after fourteen years."

Pedagogic Interventions

According to Pratham's Annual Survey of Education Report 2007, there is a considerable decline in the percentage of out-of-school children in the age-group of 6-14 from 6.6 per cent in 2006 to 4.2 per cent in 2007. However, the learning achievement of such children needs to be studied. The child, who is taken back to the school, has to cope up within a short span of time to come up to the levels of his/her peers in the respective classes. This is a very difficult task both for the child and the teacher. It is a challenging task for the teachers to take the child from initial level of learning to the desired level of appropriate class. It also provides opportunity to integrate experiential learning of the child with formal schooling. For example, Rita studied upto class-II and then discontinued for three years. She is now twelve years old. Now, she will be given admission in class-VI. Let us see what Rita brings to the classroom or what are her major assets?

1. Experience of previous schooling;
2. Previous learning experienced through interaction with the real world outside the classroom, which a regular child of her age may not have acquired;
3. Better problem-solving ability;
4. Experience due to age maturity;
5. Better psychomotor control;
6. Experience of socio-cultural milieu because of spending more time in the society;
7. Better socialization process; and
8. Better use of formal learning in real-life situation.

Nevertheless, the child will still face some serious problems, which cannot be undermined. Some of these are:

1. She may not understand the contents, which are taught in the age appropriate class;
2. She may not relate the contents taught in the classroom with the outside reality;
3. She may not cope up with the school environment, peer groups and teachers;
4. She may feel depressed or frustrated and suffer from an inferiority complex;
5. Teachers may have low expectations from her;
6. Poor performance in the classroom; or
7. She may have adjustment problems with peer groups, friends and teachers.

In such a situation, teachers and educational planners should think of the strategies and intervention to bring such children to the school and make them to cope up with the mainstream education. They may not have adequate training or awareness to deal with such children. They must be competent enough to take advantage of experiential learning of such learners. Both face-to-face and distance mode may be used for developing the competency of the teachers to deal with such children.

Needed Pedagogic Reform

The curriculum and textbooks need to be intrinsically connected with the child's life outside the school, and should reinforce the child's pride in her language, society and way of life, at the same time affording opportunities for learning about the wider world. The Bridge Course for out-of-school children should normally be a short-term course transacted in a child-friendly and playway method. Learning for children, especially during the process of mainstreaming (completion of Bridge course) should be joyful, meaningful and interesting. It should be interdisciplinary, integrating practical, art work and conceptual elements. The teaching-learning activities should help in learning and creative thinking. Activity-based methods, story-telling, learning through playway, puppet shows, drama, role-plays should be encouraged. Sufficient place should be given to the experiential learning and cooperative learning. Emphasis should be given on doing things rather than merely reading and rote learning. Curriculum should be structured in such a way that it makes such children feel that they are part of the system and have the freedom to express their voice.

It may be achieved through either the formal system or the non-formal system, a bridge-cum-condensed course may be provided to the child to cope up with the formal system. There is a need to develop the profile of each of such children. Planners may also think of the adoption of individualized instruction for such children. Such children could be at grade two level in social science, grade four level in mathematics, or grade five level in language. The child may be using the operations of addition, subtraction, multiplication and division in day-to-day life problem solving. But she may not express it through writing. Similarly, she may have knowledge about family, neighbourhood, community, etc. but may not express it in written form. Hence, bridge course should be modular in nature and according to the needs of the learners. Fragmented subject-based approach may not be congenial for such children. Instead, an integrated approach may be followed, where formal (classroom), informal (community) and non-formal (bridge course) learning is integrated.

Language of Instruction

If the language of instruction in a school in a tribal area is the State language, the child will find the school environment alienating. The analysis of educational indicators shows that majority of tribal children drop out of the primary school due to difference in the school and home language. Teaching materials and textbooks are developed in a language, which students do not understand; content of books and syllabi ignore the students' own knowledge and experience and focus only on the dominant language and culture. Not understanding the school language and course content, children are unable to cope and end up repeating grades and eventually drop out.

Educational research has shown that the mother tongue is the best medium of instruction. Support from all quarters interested in and accountable to a pluralistic social order is needed in this regard. The states, which have shown some initiative in this regard, also need to be supported. Native speakers may be recruited as teachers to teach in the local language. Educational materials and textbooks may be developed in local languages using resources available within the community. Resource centres in tribal dominated states may be established for providing training, academic and other technical support for the development of pedagogic tools and education materials catering to multilingual situations. Special training in multilingual education may be organized for teachers. Teachers should be sensitized about tribal cultures and practices. Local knowledge may be incorporated in the curriculum and textbooks. Community members may be involved in school activities to reduce social distance between the school and the community. Special training may be organized for non-tribal teachers to work in tribal areas, including knowledge of the tribal dialect.

Social Access

If teachers in the school are not sensitized to actively dispel traditional perceptions regarding gender or caste roles, they cannot help girls, children from disadvantaged groups and weaker sections to pursue their education, which is equitable and free of anxiety. The teachers' own patterns of communication with children: seating arrangements in the classroom, allocation of work between children reinforce or dispel societal perceptions about role and place of girls or children from SC/ST and minority communities. School access, therefore, demands not merely physical access to a *neighbourhood school*, but also social access by way of *addressing all exclusionary practices* in the school, especially those based on caste, class, gender and special needs.

First Generation School Goers

The government schools have a high proportion of first generation school goers and children from marginalised communities. Teachers need to be sensitive to the fact that the home environments of many of these children may not facilitate 'time-dot' punctuality of children or homework or revision of school work. If these are perceived as 'lapses' and the child is punished or the school does not help such children cope with learning, the child is likely to feel discouraged and drop out of formal schooling. Teachers and educational administrators must be sensitive to these children, and ensure that, given their difficult circumstances, the children are enabled to participate in and complete elementary education.

Social Mapping

The provision of schooling facilities at appropriate locations is an essential prerequisite to universal elementary education. But mere provision of schooling facility is insufficient to ensure that all children attend school and participate in the learning process. The school may be there, but children may not attend; they may drop out after a few months; or maybe, stay absent for too many days and cannot cope with the learning load. School mapping exercises will have to incorporate social mapping and should be undertaken with community involvement to ensure that all children, who cannot access school for social, cultural and economic reasons, are enabled to do so. Then only all children, irrespective of their caste, religion or gender would be provided education of reasonable quality.

Flexible Academic Cycle

The education of many children is often interrupted because of a mismatch in the academic calendar and school timings with the life pattern of the community. Centralised decisions mandate uniform academic calendar and school timings. It does not take into consideration context-specific needs like social and economic events, such as festivals, seasons for sowing, harvesting. As a result, there is irregular attendance and participation of children in the schooling process. For example, there are children in urban areas, who are required to fetch water for their families from a public facility, which may delay their attendance in schools. Similarly, in rural areas, some children have to fetch water from far off places, collect fire wood or are engaged in some other activity, which may marginally delay their arrival in school, or some children would require a short break during school hours to carry lunch for their family members working in the fields. There may be children, who would want to leave a little early on Friday for prayers. There is a need for decentralisation of processes and procedures in order to address the locale-specific needs to harmonize the academic and community calendars.

Girls' Education

With regard to access and retention, the focus would be on older girls, where the need is the greatest. Support measures that address economic, academic and social dimensions that lead to drop-out would need to be planned as more cohesive interventions. Measures may include transport, escorts, counselling, helping them negotiate domestic work burdens, community support mechanisms, and academic support depending on the nature of the problem.

Exciting Activities§

Junior Learners: A few exciting activities, involving playway technology, word games, use of flash cards, work sheets, and individual skill composition, adventure reporting, etc. based on the rich experience of the DIET faculty and experts rightly deserve attention to help out-of-school children interested to pursue their education in a joyful environment in their respective learning centres at schools. Some of these are included here as suggestive of many others.

Learning Alphabets

1. Match the capital letters with small letters in the following table:

A	d
B	i
C	l
D	n
E	c
F	a
G	b
H	j
I	f
J	h
K	e
L	p
M	g
N	k
O	q
P	r

1 Contributed by Dr. Sharda Kumari, Sr. Lecturer DIET, R.K. Puram, New Delhi.

Q	t
R	m
S	o
T	w
U	v
V	s
W	y
X	u
Y	z
Z	x

2. Match the pictures with correct alphabet (first letter of the word):

R	
D	
B	
C	
T	
F	

Understanding Colours

3. Write the colours of the following articles opposite them and colour them accordingly:

(Hints: Sun, Brinjal, Apple)

4. Colour the rainbow with the hints given (the first letter of every colour is given from top to bottom order):
V
I
B
G
Y
O
R

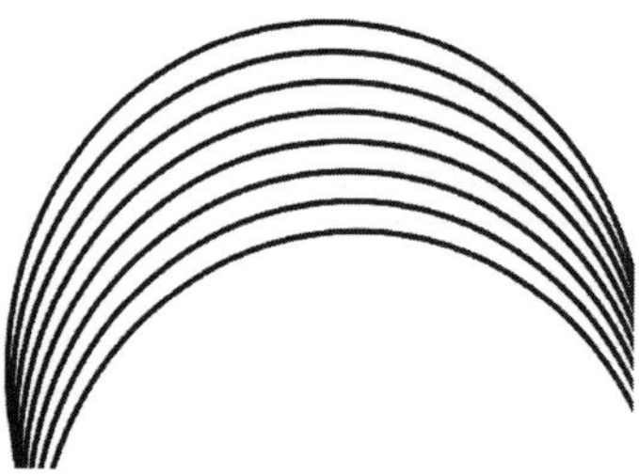

Understanding the Vocations

Teaching Material Required:

Flash cards of the photographs of professionals.

Introduction

1. Tell the students that they are going to have a group competition.
2. Divide the class into five groups
3. Make this table on the board

	Group A	*Group B*	*Group C*	*Group D*	*Group E*
Person 1	Doctor	Postman/	Policeman	Fireman/fire fighter	Shopkeeper
Person 2	Nurse	Postal workers	Police officer	Fire Officer	Barber
Tools	Medicines	Envelope	Handcuffs	Ladder/fire engine	Currency notes
Place	Hospital	Post Office	Police Station	Fire station	Market place

Some examples:

1. The doctor works in a hospital.
2. Shopkeeper is the owner of a shop. etc

Speaking: All the groups talk a lot about all these persons as give in the example.

Presentation

They write sentences about these professions using is/are/am and present indefinite.

Next, they play a quiz using their sentences, e.g.

1. This person gives us letters.
2. This person cuts our hair, etc.

Liked/Disliked Activities

1. **Activity Sheet/Work Sheet:**
   Study the following table carefully

	Aleena	*Prachi*
Running	✓	X
Washing of Clothes	✓	✓
Playing Tennis	✓	X
Reading Urdu	X	✓
Dancing	✓	X
Cooking	X	✓
Watching TV	X	✓
Riding Bicycle	X	✓

✓= likes X= dislikes (doesn't like)

Example sentence: **Aleena likes swimming, but Prachi doesn't.**

Now, in groups of six students each, talk about these two friends' likings and dislikings.

In the next step, the students talk about their own likings and disliking in pairs, e.g.

I like driving, but I don't like playing tennis.

As an extension of the activity, the learners can write five sentences about their likings and dislikings.

2. Activity Sheet/Work Sheet:

	SAHAR	*ALEENA*
Swimming	✓	X
Playing Tennis	✓	X
Reading Urdu	X	✓
Dancing	✓	X
Cooking	X	✓
Watching TV	X	✓

✓= likes X= dislikes

Example sentence: **Sahar likes swimming, but Aleena doesn't.**

Learning Tasks and Skills

Activity

1. Listening Skill
2. Link to Learning Objective— Listening for specific information—Simile
3. Assessment Objective—Formative
4. Materials—Honeysuckle—Textbook in English for Class VI
5. Name of The Lesson/Poem—Kite
6. Time—1 Period, 35 Minutes
7. Task Type -Understand what simile is and its usage.
8. Procedure

- Explain the objective, assessment criteria and how to grade the students
- Give instructions for the task
- The teacher can explain to the class, what a simile is. 'A simile is a way of describing something by comparing it to something else, often using the word "like" or "as." For example, *"He is as brave as a lion."* The word simile is pronounced SIM-il-ee.
- The teacher can revise adjectives and take five minutes recapitulation on adjectives.
- The teacher writes the list of adjectives on the board, covering the whole board. The list is as follows; the teacher can add on to the list and give more words according to the understanding of their students—tall, short, angry, happy, ugly, beautiful, old, young, wet, dry, hard, soft, smart, etc.
- Now organise the students into pairs.
- Ask them to discuss the various options of making similes. The teacher can facilitate for five to eight minutes. Then, discuss with the whole class.
- The students are instructed to now choose any two adjective words and write down a simile for each word. Each student will give one example and the rest of the students will listen, comment and discuss.

Learning Language through Pictures

Activity—Listen and Draw

Objective

Listen with comprehension.
Express fluently by reading the picture.
Encourage VISUAL learners.

TIME -20 MINUTES

Advance Preparation

Pencil, Eraser, Coloured Pencils/Colours;

Procedure

1. Divide the class in small groups of three students each.
2. Ask each group to decide the names of the members who will draw, write and read the passage.
3. Ask them to Listen to the passage carefully and draw the picture:

A BIG FRUIT BASKET IS LYING ON THE TABLE. THERE ARE FOUR BANANAS AND THREE APPLES IN THE BASKET. IT ALSO HAS A SMALL BUNCH OF GRAPES AND A PAPAYA TOO. TWO APPLES ARE LYING OUTSIDE THE BASKET. A "HAPPY DIWALI' CARD IS TIED TO THE HANDLE OF THE BASKET. THERE IS A GIRL STANDING NEXT TO THE TABLE. SHE HAS TWO APPLES IN HER HANDS.

4. After they have drawn, make them tell the class what they have drawn.
5. The other groups will listen to them carefully and will try to find out if the description matches the original passage.

Tick the correct picture identifying the adjective.

1. warm

2. strong

3. slow

4. sleepy

5. scary

6. rich

7. poor

8. painful

9. old

10. noisy

11. hungry

12. heavy

13. handsome

14. full

15. sick

16. fat

17. fast

18. far

19. famous

20. difficult

21. cute

22. cool

23. cold

24. busy

25. bad

26. angry

Learners work in groups. They talk about these pictures. Now, the learners make sentences using these adjectives orally only. As an extension of the activity, the learners write sentences in their groups.

Understanding via Star Games

Three facts about me

- One of the following is wrong. Find out, through skilful questioning, which one is wrong (no direct questions).
- Travelling and Driving is my passion
- I can predict your future through your handwriting
- I have never visited a European country
- I have been to the USA twice

Activity	The star of my life
Time	45 minutes
Advance preparation	The RP will draw his/her own 'star of my life' writing some hints about his own life, achievements, marriage, parents, children, countries visited or any other notable things on all corners of the star.

Centre of the star can be used for writing the most important thing of his life. Like P....... for parents, or C...... for country etc.

Objectives:

- Making rapport with the fellow participants.
- Gathering common information in an interesting way.
- Communication in English—speaking and listening.
- Sharing personal information.
- Getting to know you/each other.
- Using the simple structure 'is/are/am in an interesting way.
- Using the structure 'may' for probability.

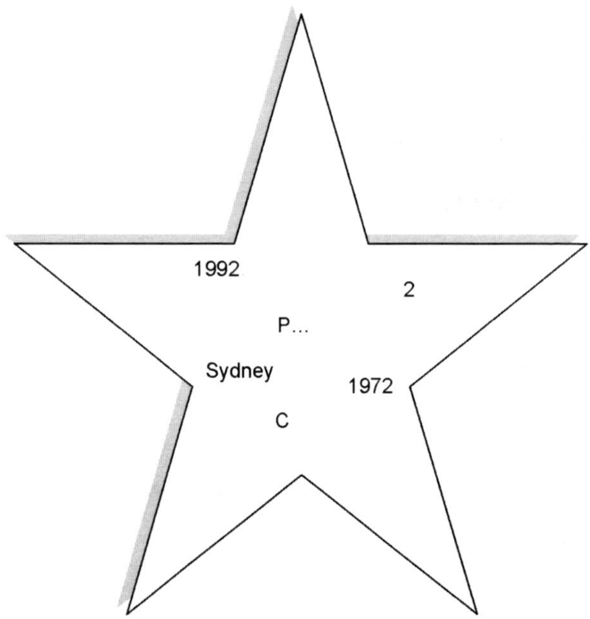

Now, showing your star to the participants, ask them to guess the things or events of your life, e.g.

What could 1972 be ?	It is the year of my birth.
What is 2?	It is the number of children I have.
Sydney ?	It is the place from where I graduated.

1992?	It is the year when I graduated.
P?	It stands for parents
C?	It stand for the country I visited.

Activities for Intermediate Learners

Prepared and contributed by		*Dr. Khaleeq Ahmad*
Activity name	:	Rescue
Time	:	15-25 mintues
Grouping of students	:	5-8
Materials	:	none

Learning Speaking Skills

Objective: *Speaking*

Language functions—Stating an opinion, giving and asking for reasons, agreeing and disagreeing, comparisons

Instructions

Procedure

1. The teacher explains the situation: (2-3 minutes)
   The earth is doomed to perish. Everything is going to be destroyed in the next two days due to radiation. Some aliens from another planet have come to rescue, but they can carry only twelve people and shift them to some other planet, which is very similar to our earth. These twelve people will start a new world of human race there. Imagine you are the only authority to decide, who may be rescued. Think of a list of criteria, which you would use in your decision and why. Discuss in your group and come to a conclusion.
2. Each group discusses the problem and tries to work out a list. (5-8 minutes)
3. Each group presents its list of criteria to the class. The lists are discussed. (8-10 minutes)

Variations

1. The task can be made more specific like, ten criteria.
2. Up to 100 marks can be awarded on all counts like—appearance, intelligence, fertility, physical fitness, age, gender, etc.
3. To make the task more challenging, a list of 10 most important things to be carried along can also be asked to prepare.

Stages (please include suggested times):

Stage 1. (2-3 minutes)
Stage 2. (5-8 minutes)
Stage 3. (8-10 minutes)

Look and Identify

This activity will be done through role play.

- Five or six children will volunteer themselves to work as a group.
- Take a few slips of paper in your hand in which various drawings of park, birthday celebration, classroom, games are given.
- If the group picks up the slip of 'park', ask them to present the scene of park without telling rest of the students about the situation. Tell them that this will be a mime (silent play), they should not speak even a single word.
- Give them five minutes to prepare.
- When the scene will develop and other children identify it, you will say 'statue' (All the children will stand still in mid-action)

Pointing towards each child, you may ask questions about the actions being performed by him/her, for example:

- What is Rita doing? Rita is skipping.

- What are Asim and Manu doing?Asim and Manu are playing with a ball, etc.
- Write the responses of the children on the blackboard.
- What scene is being depicted by the children?

Now you may ask more questions related to that scene, e.g. if the scene is of a park, then

(a) What else happens in a park?
(b) Which are the other things seen in a park?

Let children encircle naming words out of these and underline the action words.

Other groups will perform actions in a similar way.

Learning Word Web Games

- Observation of immediate environment
- Naming different objects and recording them
- Discussion on the things recorded
- You may write a word in a circle on the board and ask the children to speak out other words related to it, thus, creating a word web, e.g., a word web for the word 'sky' may come up like this.

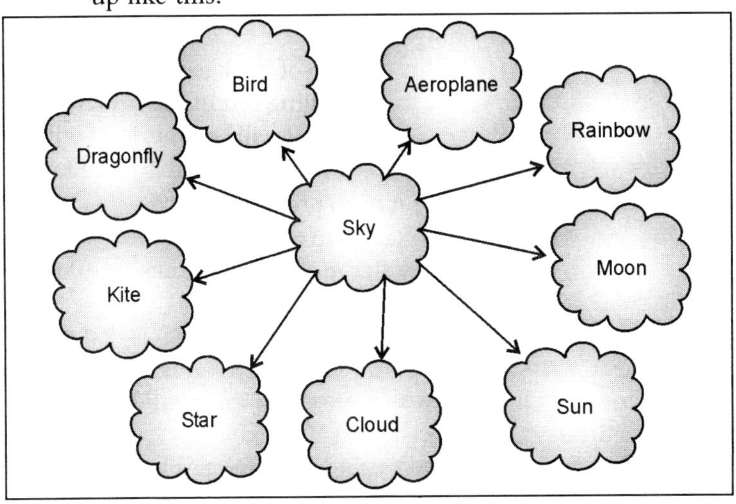

Children may speak a number of words, besides these. You may also help the students to come up with more words. A discussion may be organised on various words spoken by them. For example—

- Where have you seen a rainbow?
- How does it look like?
- What is the colour of the sky?
- When do you see the moon?
- Which of the things written are human made?

A number of such questions can be framed to familiarise children with their surroundings.

Just a Minute

- Recalling previous experiences and observations.
- Classifying the animals into domestic or wild; and food items into raw or cooked
- Singular or plural, opposite words

Divide the class in two groups 'A' and 'B'. You will announce a few (5 -10) letters e.g. 'P' in the class. Group 'A' will name one animal and bird starting with a specific letter 'P', e.g., Pig and Parrot and Group 'B' will name one fruit, vegetable and food item starting with the letter e.g. Potato and Poha.

Give a few (5 -10) chances to both the groups. Give equal chances to both the groups. The group giving more answers correctly will be the winner.

Enlist the names spoken by children on blackboard under the above mentioned two categories.

Once the list is developed, children may be asked to classify these into the following categories in their notebooks.

- The food items that are obtained from animals and plants.
- Food items eaten as cooked, raw or both.
- Birds and animals, which are domestic or wild.

(If children find it difficult to name the things from a specific letter, you may even ask them to name any animal, bird or food item)

This game can also be played with:

- Some action words and describing words
- Opposite, Gender
- Singular, Plural, etc.
- A word chain game can also be played where one child will speak one word starting with the last letter of the word spoken by the other child.

Understanding the Movement of Time Dial

You Always Care for us

- Expression through role play about theme related to conservation of natural environment.
- Identification of different actions
- Classification of different actions under two categories
- Sensitisation towards preservation and conservation of natural resources.

Let one child enact a tree. Some other children will enact different actions, such as watering the tree, one tired traveller sitting and sleeping under its shadow, feeling hungry and plucking a fruit from it, plucking leaves mischievously, swinging from a tree branch, cutting the tree, pelting stones at the tree, playing around the tree, scribbling on a tree, etc.

After each action, the tree child will use different expressions to express sorrow, pain, joy, relief, etc.

The rest of the class will guess the actions and describe them.

Rina is watering the tree.
Shyam is cutting the tree.

Where is the Shadow

- Sketching the outline of the shadows at different intervals of a day

- Observation and comparison of the size of shadows with respect to time, i.e., morning, evening, afternoon, etc.

Place or fix a crowman at such a place in the school where its shadow varies throughout the day. You can even choose a plant or pole or any other such object. Let the children observe at different intervals during the school time and sketch the outline of the crowman on the ground using a chalk. Let them observe the variations. Now, ask them:

1. At what time, the shadow of the crowman was the smallest?
2. At what time the shadow of the crowman was the largest?

Let them repeat this activity for two-three days and authenticate their conclusions. Help them relate the size of shadows with the different intervals of a day.

If possible, a visit to an observatory may be arranged. The working of the Sun Dial may be explained.

6

Pedagogical Inputs at Elementary Stage

Pedagogy, the science and art of education, specifically instructional, is the study of teaching methods and theories about the way learning takes place. In the traditional teaching-learning process, the teacher is considered as the provider of knowledge and students the recipients, supposed to memorise the knowledge and reproduce the same in the examination. This process ignores the methods of inquisitiveness of the learners and their ability to construct new knowledge.

But things are not the same now. Students' engagement today is critical in the classroom as regards school-related knowledge. They are not just young people for whom adults should devise solutions. They are critical observers of their own conditions and needs as well as participants in problem-solving related to their education and future opportunities. They are aware that their experiences and perceptions are important and that they possess the courage to develop their mental skills needed to think and reason independently. Their capacities, learning abilities and knowledge base that they possess and bring to school from outside due to knowledge explosion is important to further enhance their learning process. This is true for children from underprivileged backgrounds, too, especially girls, as the world they inhabit and the realities they are faced with, are unrepresented in the school knowledge.

How do Children Learn?

Children are natural learners. They construct their own knowledge.

They actively engage themselves with the world around them, exploring, responding, inventing and working things out and making their own meaning.

Modern pedagogy, strongly influenced by the cognitivism of Piaget, the social-interactionist theories of Bruner and the social and cultural theories of Vygotsky have laid a new foundation for pedagogy, where sequential development of individual mental processes such as recognize, recall, analyze, reflect, apply, create, understand and evaluate are scaffolded. Students learn as they internalize the procedures, organization and structures encountered in social contexts as to their own schema. They learn to integrate their prior knowledge with the new knowledge and also develop their metacognition, that is, the ability to learn how to learn. The National Council of Educational Research and Training (NCERT)'s National Curriculum Framework (NCF, 2005), too, emphasizes on the 'learner-centered approaches' to achieve objectives of the curriculum.

Learner-Centred Pedagogy

'Learner-centred' pedagogy means giving primacy to learners' experiences, their voices and their active participation. This pedagogy involves/requires us to plan learning in keeping with the children's psychological development and interests, responding to their physical, cultural and social preferences and needs.

Our school pedagogic practices, learning tasks and the texts we create for learners tend to focus on the socialisation of children and on the 'receptive' features of children's learning. Children's voices and experiences generally do not find expression in the classroom. Instead, we need to nurture and build on their active and creative capabilities—their inherent interest in making meaning, in relating to the world in 'real' ways through acting on it and creating, and in relating to other humans. Learning should be active and social in its character. Pedagogy used should be such that it must enable children to find their voices, nurture their curiosity—to do things, to ask questions and to pursue investigations, sharing and integrating their experiences with school knowledge—rather than their ability to reproduce textual knowledge.

Children will learn only in an atmosphere where they feel they are valued. Our schools still do not convey this to all children. The association of learning with fear, discipline and stress rather than enjoyment and satisfaction, is detrimental to learning. Our children need to feel that each one of them, their homes, communities, languages and culture are valuable as resources for experience to be analysed and enquired into at school; that their diverse capabilities are accepted; that all of them have the ability and the right to learn and to access knowledge and skills; and that adult society regards them as capable of the best.

The ways in which children learn and develop vary greatly from child to child. There are a vast number of children's learning theories in circulation that raise issues of student development and learning. No single theory has been adequate to fully explain learning and/or development thus far. Hence, there is the need to explore a viable learner-centred pedagogy.

Critical Pedagogy

NCF-2005 also talks about critical pedagogy, a philosophy of education described first by Paulo Freire. It ventures for an opportunity to learn by reflecting critically on issues in terms of their political, social, economic and moral aspects. It entails the acceptance of multiple views on social issues and a commitment to democratic forms of interaction in which our schools function. A critical framework helps children to see social issues from different perspectives and understand how such issues are connected to life. For instance, understanding of democracy as a way of life can be chartered through a path where children reflect on how they regard others (e.g., friends, neighbours, the opposite sex, elders, etc.)? How they make choices (e.g., activities, play, friends, career, etc.)? And how they cultivate the ability to make decisions? Likewise, issues related to human rights, caste, religion and gender can be critically reflected on by children in order to see how these issues are connected to their everyday experiences and also how different forms of inequalities become compounded and perpetuated. Critical pedagogy facilitates collective decision-making through open discussion and by encouraging and recognising multiple views.

Participatory Learning

Participatory learning and teaching have a definite and valued place in classroom. While class participation is a powerful strategy, it loses its pedagogic edge when it is ritualised. It merely becomes an instrument to enable teachers to meet their own ends. True participation starts from the experiences of both students and teachers. When children and teachers share and reflect on their individual and collective experiences without fear of judgement, it gives them opportunities to learn about others who may not be a part of their own social reality. This enables them to understand, instead of fearing, them.

If children's social experiences are to be brought into the classroom, it is inevitable that issues of conflict will need to be addressed. Conflict is an inescapable part of children's lives. They constantly encounter situations that call for moral assessment and action, whether in relation to subjective experiences of conflict involving the self, family and society, or in dealing with exposure to violent conflict in the contemporary world. To use conflict as a pedagogic strategy is to enable children to deal with conflict and facilitate awareness of its nature and its role in their lives. Learners must be encouraged to comment, compare and think about elements that exist in their own environment.

A pedagogy insensitive to gender, class, caste and global inequalities does not merely affirm different individual and collective experiences, but also locates these within larger structures of power and raises questions, such as: who is allowed to speak for whom? Whose knowledge is the most valued?

This requires evolving different strategies for different learners. For example, encouraging speaking up in class may be important for some children, while for others, it may be learning to listen to others. The role of teachers is to provide a safe space for children to express themselves, and simultaneously to build in certain forms of interactions. They need to step out of the role of 'moral authority' and learn to listen with empathy and without judgement, and to enable children to listen to each other. While consolidating and constructively stretching the limits of the learner's understanding, they need to be conscious of how differences are expressed.

Women and dalit activists have used songs as a powerful medium for discussion, comments and analysis. Repositories of knowledge exist in different media forms; hence, all these forms, whether television programmes, advertisements, songs, paintings, etc. need to be brought into the classroom to help create a dynamic interaction among learners themselves.

An atmosphere of trust would make the classroom a safe space, where children can share experiences; where conflict can be acknowledged and constructively questioned; and where resolutions, however tentative, be mutually worked out. In particular, for girls and children from the under-privileged social groups, schools and classrooms should be spaces for discussing the processes of decision-making, for questioning the basis of their decisions, and for making informed choices.

In learner-centred classrooms, students use their own learning strategies. They may use problem-solving, experiential learning, investigatory approach, social inquiry and concept mapping for constructing and validating new ideas.

Experiential Learning

Experiential learning involves four steps, namely: concrete experience; observation and reflection; formulation of new concepts/ ideas; and validating new ideas. The process of learning starts with action and analyzing the effect of that action. The learner would then reflect upon and provide adequate explanation. Generalisation and development of theory may involve action over a range of circumstances and expressing the result in a symbolic form. This type of learning allows for divergent learning styles in the classroom.

Problem-Solving

Problem-solving approach helps in developing higher cognitive abilities of thinking as well as transfer and application of knowledge to new situations. Learning is more meaningful and permanent using this approach. Here, students are active participants in the construction of new knowledge. Students formulate hypotheses, suggest alternate solutions, conduct experiments, draw generalizations, compare their findings and results with those of others, verify and validate their own ideas. Students develop thinking, observational and enquiry skills.

Investigatory Approach

Investigatory approach develops the abilities to formulate hypotheses, measuring, planning, enquiry and communication. Students pose questions, plan out and investigate, hypothesise, predict and evaluate. This approach is very useful in learning science and social science subjects.

Concept Mapping

Concept mapping is useful in learning about the structure of knowledge and understanding the process of knowledge construction. It involves *meta-learning*, that is, *learning about learning*. The steps involved in concept mapping are selecting the key concepts and sub-concepts, linking the concepts and sub-concepts through prepositions and making meaning out of horizontal and vertical linkages. Concept maps help in understanding the existing concepts of the learners. These can also be used to diagnose the gaps in learning.

Social Inquiry Approach

Social inquiry is a useful learner-centred approach. It requires students to collect, analyse and interpret data, draw generalizations and develop theories and concepts on the basis of empirical research-based data. Field survey and research involve community participation.

Creative Writing

This method can be used to teach all subjects like language, science, social sciences and mathematics. Creative writing helps in developing the abilities of reporting, arguing, explaining, persuading, reflecting, coping and evaluating. It involves free expression of thought, feelings and emotions. It involves all those methods where learner's own initiatives and efforts are involved in learning.

Peer Learning

Peer learning is an educational practice in which students interact with other students to attain educational goals. In this context, it can be compared to the practices that go by the name of cooperative learning. It takes place both in formal and informal learning contexts. Many schools now promote instructional methods involving 'active' learning that present opportunities for students to formulate their own questions, discuss issues, explain their viewpoints and engage in cooperative learning by working in teams on problems and projects. 'Peer learning' is a form of cooperative learning that enhances the value of student-student interaction and results in various advantageous learning outcomes.

To realise the benefits of peer learning, teachers must provide 'intellectual scaffolding'.

Example: Teachers should select some discussion topics that all students are likely to have some relevant knowledge of; they also should raise questions/issues that prompt students towards more sophisticated levels of thinking. Collaborative processes are required to be devised to get all group members to participate meaningfully. To facilitate successful peer learning, teachers may choose any strategy: like forming *Buzz group* (A large group of students sub-divided into smaller groups of 4-5 students to consider the issues surrounding a problem. After about 20 minutes of discussion, one member of each sub-group presents the findings of the sub-group to the whole group); or *Affinity group* (Group of 4-5 students can be assigned particular tasks or motivated to choose tasks of their own choice, depending upon their likes, but related to the theme of study and discuss with their team members or community members outside the school and present the outcome to the whole class).

Some *Critique groups* can also be formulated and they can be assigned a discussion topic for a class and the other groups constituted as 'critics' will observe, offer comments and evaluate the sub-group's presentation. At the end of a unit, students can be given short answer questions by the teacher and students would be required to answer and justify their answers. After working on the questions individually, students compare their answers with each other's. Critique sessions, role-play debates, case studies and integrated projects are other exciting and effective teaching strategies that stir students' enthusiasm and encourage peer learning.

Collaborative Learning

Collaborative learning is a situation in which two or more people learn or attempt to learn something together. Collaborative learning is based on the model that knowledge can be created within a population where members actively interact by sharing experiences and take on asymmetry roles. Collaborative learning refers to methodologies and environments in which learners engage in a common task where each individual depends on and is accountable to each other. Collaborative learning occurs because individual participation in learning occurs on a horizontal plane where children and adults are equal. Collaborative learning occurs when children and adults engage in play, work and other activities together.

Cooperative Learning

Students work in groups to complete the assigned tasks collectively toward academic goals. Unlike individual learning, which can be competitive in nature, students learning cooperatively capitalize on one another's resources and skills (asking one another for information, evaluating one another's ideas, monitoring one another's work, etc.) Everyone succeeds when the group succeeds. Ross and Smyth (1995) described successful cooperative learning tasks as intellectually demanding, creative, open-ended, involving higher order thinking tasks.

7

Capacity Building and ICT Integration

Programmes for capacity building of elementary school teachers can be divided into two categories: Face-to-Face and Distance Education Mode programmes. The major programmes and activities undertaken by the Centre and State Governments are briefly presented here.

Face-to-Face Programmes

Orientation to Develop Locale-specific Materials

The curriculum and textbooks need to be intrinsically connected with the child's life outside the school. Curriculum should reinforce the child's pride in her language, society and way of life. Hence, teacher trainees both at pre-service and in-service levels should be oriented to develop locale-specific materials, easily understandable with pictures, illustrations, citing local examples. Workshops for teachers may be organized to develop primers in local languages. Teaching-learning materials suitable to local context may be developed in workshops. Modular bridge courses taking into account the locale specific context may be developed through workshop mode during in-service training. Educational materials, textbooks, etc. may be developed in local languages, using resources available within the community.

Pedagogical Methods

The Bridge Course for out-of-school children should normally be a short-term course transacted in child-friendly and playway methods. Learning for children, especially during the process of mainstreaming (completion of Bridge Course) should be joyful, meaningful and interesting. Pedagogical methods, which are child and group-centred, such as activity-based method, learning by doing, project method, cooperative learning method, role-play, dramatization, need to be stressed in teacher education programme both at pre-service and in-service levels.

Interdisciplinary Approach

Out-of-school children, when brought to mainstream education system, come with a variety of experiences. They may be poor in learning of 3R^{s}, but may be rich in social and field experiences. These experiences are an asset for the child, which may further be explored. Hence, the approach should be interdisciplinary, integrating practical, art work and conceptual elements. Hence, teachers should be oriented about the importance of interdisciplinary, approach instead of subject-centric approach. There should be sufficient opportunities at pre-service level to practise such an approach. Take an example of 'Water'. Subject-centric approach will give a fragmented view of water. In science, the child will learn about the chemical formula of water, its composition, water cycle, water pollution, etc. An out-of-school child may find difficulty in understanding it. However, when 'water' is seen from interdisciplinary perspective, the child will learn about economic, political and social issues related to water and enjoy them as day-to-day experiences.

Exposure to Community Work

Mere provision of schooling facility is insufficient to ensure that all children attend school and participate in the learning process. The school may be there, but children may not attend; they may drop out after a few months; or may be absent for too many days and cannot cope with the learning load. Hence, exposure to community work should be an integral part of pre-service teacher education programmes. Trainees should go to community, interact with the members, collect data regarding enrolment, drop-outs, etc.; problems and issue; and prepare a project. The academic calendar may not adequately reflect the community's economic and social circumstances on children's attendance and participation. Hence, the trainee should be trained to prepare locale-specific academic calendar taking into consideration context-specific needs like social and economic events, such as festivals, the sowing season, harvesting, etc.

Project to deal with a Drop-out Child

A project to deal with a drop-out child, who requires identification, community level school mapping; organisation of special training of flexible duration to enable the child to be at par with other children; motivating for actual admission of the child in the age-appropriate class on completion of training; etc., should be given to pupil teachers at the pre-service level training.

Resource Centres in Tribal Dominated States

Educational research has shown that mother tongue is the best medium of instruction. Support from all quarters interested in and accountable to a pluralistic social order is needed in this regard. The states, which have shown some initiative in this regard, will also need to be supported. Native speakers may be recruited as teachers to teach in the local languages. Resource centres in tribal dominated states may be established for providing training, academic and other technical support for the development of pedagogic tools and educational materials catering to multilingual situations. Special training in multilingual education may be organized for teachers, and they should be sensitized about tribal culture and practices. Local knowledge may be incorporated in the curriculum and textbooks. Special training may be organized for non-tribal teachers to work in tribal areas, including knowledge of the tribal dialect.

Social Survey

Social survey on caste, class, gender and special needs should be part of practical work during pre-service training programme. Strong elements of understanding child labour, the role of the education system and how discriminatory attitudes will increase drop-out rates and lead to entrenched problems of child labour need to be incorporated in it.

Understanding of Child Labour Issues

Understanding of issues related to child labour is essential during teacher education programmes. Series of teacher training workshops on child labour may be organized to create awareness about these problems. Training may include: a strong focus on child labour; short but intensive training periods; and in-service training workshops for training trainers on child labour issues and pedagogical skills to subsequently reach larger groups of teachers. The approach should be both creative and flexible. Experience has shown that adjusting training in terms of content, length and focus is possible without compromising the core message on child labour.

Manuals and Handbooks for Teachers

National and State level agencies, NGOs should develop manuals, handbooks, and Teaching Learning Materials (TLMs) for teachers and resource persons to raise awareness about the importance of mainstreaming out-of-school children. Pedagogical methods to deal with children, who are either out-of school; brought to school; or those, who may drop out from the school in future should be there in the handbooks. Issues may cover the nature of child labour; child labour in relation to the educational system; how to identify students at-risk in the classroom; classroom management skills; how to improve student learning in the classroom; child to child programme techniques; conflict resolution and social skills; counselling needs of working children; and remedial teaching.

Teacher Education through Distance Mode

The distance mode has the capacity to reach millions of learners through the modern communication technologies. Perraton *et al.* (2007) indicated that ODL is increasingly being used to:

- Provide cost-effective pre-service and in-service teacher education;
- Support school-based pre-service and continuing professional development programmes for teachers;
- Upgrade unqualified teachers and enable qualified teachers to acquire higher teaching qualifications;
- Provide teachers in remote or rural areas with access to professional training, thereby meeting their continuing professional development needs; and
- Ensure quick dissemination of information to large number of teachers about curriculum innovations, new teaching methodologies, practices and new professional standards for teaching.

Radio and television have proved their worth in disseminating not only information and knowledge, but also developing skills. Through audio/video programmes, teachers would be provided content as well as pedagogic inputs besides sensitizing parents about the importance of schooling and education.

Radio has been valuable in reaching out to a large number of teachers and in providing in-service training. Radio broadcasts can be effectively used to support print-based open and distance delivery of teacher education programmes. Community radio can be used to create awareness and training of teachers and community about the importance of bringing out-of-school children and children at-risk at local level. Community radio is a radio station owned, run and maintained by a community. It encourages expression and participation of local community and values local culture. Its purpose is to give a voice to those without voice, to marginalized groups and to communities far from large cities, where the population is too small to attract commercial or large-scale State radio. Dedicated community radios for providing continuous professional development of teachers at local levels may be established with support from the government. Radio stations may operate from DIETs, CTEs and IASEs. Local pool of resources may be created and used for professional development of teachers.

Tailor-made self-learning materials alongwith user-manuals may be developed for creating awareness and pedagogical inputs needed for mainstreaming out-of-school children and children at-risk. Teachers may be encouraged to practise in-text activities given in the materials.

Past experiences show that tele-conferencing is not able to attract much interactivity. There is a need to combine teleconferencing with the workshops organized for training at different locations. Workshops can be organized at different locations in the country with a facilitating resource person. This can make teleconferencing more interactive and enable different workshop participants to interact with experts.

Sarva Shiksha Abhiyan (SSA)

Sarva Shiksha Abhiyan (SSA) is a national programme to realise the goals of Universalization of Elementary Education in India. It has been a national endeavour for which both the Central and the State Governments have been devising various measures through different modes.

The Distance Education Programme (DEP) has been envisaged as a national component and a major area of intervention in Sarva Shiksha Abhiyan, which focuses on 'strengthening training through open distance learning'. DEP was established by the Government of India on the 1st of July 2003 as an upgraded project of the erstwhile DEP-DPEP (Distance Education Programme—District Primary Education Programme), which had been in operation in 18 States and seven UTs. This national project aimed at providing need-based, locale-specific in-service training to teachers, resource persons, DIET faculty and other functionaries involved in the elementary education programme.

DEP plays a major role in providing technical support to the states in building capacity among institutions and people at national, state, district and sub-district levels to design, develop, produce and deliver distance learning inputs and materials in a recurrent manner. Under the DEP-SSA project, various initiatives like appointing Distance Education Coordinators, constitution of the State Resource Groups for Distance Education Programme (SRG-DEP), holding SRG meetings for identifying training needs, planning of activities, capacity building activities in distance learning material development and distance delivery modes have been undertaken in some States. It has been maximally utilizing various means of communication—Print, Audio and Video material, Teleconferencing, Computer etc. to achieve the target of quality elementary education.

DEP-SSA Interventions

Teacher training is an important area in the Government of India's Sarva Shiksha Abhiyan (SSA) programme for Universalizing Elementary Education (UEE) in the country. SSA emphasizes on quality training programme for large number of in-service and untrained elementary school teachers. IGNOU, being the nodal agency for imparting quality training to all stakeholders of elementary education in the country, to this end DEP-SSA is carved out as a component within SSA under the overall leadership of IGNOU. The DEP-SSA endeavours the convergence of all efforts for providing quality elementary education to all. Its major focus is on:

- Need-based and locale-specific capacity building of institutions and personnel at national, state, district and sub-district levels;
- Providing technical support in designing, developing and delivering distance learning materials for training elementary school teachers and other functionaries;
- Strengthening institutions by creating infrastructural facilities like Direct Reception Sites (DRS), Satellite Interactive Terminals (Downlink facilities) at the State Project Offices, and other training modes even at the district levels;
- Orientation of teachers and teacher educators in the EDUSAT activities and software development;
- Providing technical and functional support in developing bridge courses for out-of-school children; and
- Monitoring SSA activities and their implementation through teleconferencing.

Since its inception, the mission for the Distance Education Programme under SSA has been to develop policy guidelines and strategies to use educational technologies for the elementary school sector. Use of ICT is augmented for training of teachers and the development of instructional materials on pedagogical and contextual issues.

The specific target groups covered by DEP-SSA are:

- Elementary teachers (untrained, trained and para teachers);
- Teacher educators;
- Block Resource Centre (BRC) and Cluster Resource Centre Coordinators; and
- State and district functionaries.

The capacity building and training of SSA functionaries is carried out by using distance learning inputs. It operates through a network of linkages with national institutions like IGNOU, NCERT, etc. and State Level institutions for designing and development of distance learning materials. DEP-SSA provides technical support in the design, development and dissemination of DL materials under the leadership of IGNOU.

The innovative use of technology is reflected in some endeavours of DEP-SSA particularly, in the year 2008-09. These include:

- Based on recommendations of National Curriculum Framework 2005, self-instructional training modules focusing on constructivist pedagogy developed in teaching of science and mathematics at upper primary level and English at primary level;
- Capacity building for development of audio-video scripts in content areas;
- Documentation of best practices (Activity Based Learning);
- Multimedia CDs prepared on English textbooks of primary classes for Goa state;
- Development of Media Resource Centre for the documentation of DL inputs by DEP-SSA;
- Video recording and editing of Teleconferences for further use;

- Online training on Wiki skills being imparted through zonal workshops; and
- Multimedia publishing e-Portal for sharing of the best practices across schools in different regions and for online support to SSA functionaries.

The DEP-SSA has created a state-level infrastructure for Distance Learning and placed a coordinator in the states, who function as intermediaries between the MHRD, GOI and the states and identify needs of the state. Many of the states have developed their own infrastructure and are using educational technologies based on local needs. The states, which have taken a lead, are Andhra Pradesh, Gujarat, Karnataka and Kerala.

Exploring the Possibilities

DEP-SSA can provide the platform for training teachers and other functionaries at the elementary level to effectively incorporate environmental concerns and issues in their classroom transactions. The capacity building programmes will empower teachers to engage their students in action-oriented project-based environment education activities. Involving students in such knowledge generation activities could lead to the documentation of some important facets of the human and physical environment. Such an exercise will greatly enhance the quality of educational experiences, which are still very authoritative and decreed by textbooks. The programme will sensitize the teachers to the requirements of education for sustainable development whether in an infused manner or as a separate subject in school.

DEP-SSA can guide the states in their needs and chart a course for their development. Some steps that can be taken in this direction as per DEP-SSA, 2009 are:

- DEP-SSA could sensitize the states about the potential of distance education for achieving EE objectives through teleconferencing and other modes;
- Exemplar materials developed by DEP-SSA, in the area of environmental Studies (EVS), could be dubbed/translated into regional languages for use by the states;

- Workshops, seminars through teleconferencing Face-to-Face mode could be organized for capacity building in the development of audio-video scripts and designing content for other delivery platforms;
- States could be mapped to identify the best practices in the use of information communication technology for imparting EE in schools;
- DEP-SSA can establish linkages with other institutions and draw on experiences of other organizations for content development, marketing skills and the utilization strategies at the school level;
- Access and utilization to be ensured at all levels;
- New technologies like mobile learning, e-learning should be explored and their utilization and impact on the school system could be done on project basis for imparting environmental concepts; and
- Collaborative learning technologies, like the DEP-SSA Wiki could be effectively used for content generation in ESD and EE, which could be shared across the states in the country. Teacher educators/master trainers could develop training modules in the area and upload on the Wiki. Multilingual Wiki portal can be used for content generation in the locale specific context.

Challenges

India, with a heterogeneous population (exceeding one billion) spread over a geographically diverse terrain, faces enormous challenges in bringing about changes in the existing school teaching-learning practices, which are still teacher-centric, examination-oriented and based on rote learning. The use of ICT in education, particularly at the school level, is still a distant dream because its diffusion throughout India's multicultural, multilingual and multi-ethnic society is not uniform. Some of the specific constraints likely to be encountered in imparting ICT enabled EE are:

- Reorientation and continuous professional development of school teachers/functionaries towards a system, which encourages students to observe and generate knowledge;

- Catering to the needs of a heterogeneous population, which includes millions of teachers and students, operating under severe constraints.
- Need to link all efforts to local problems, concerns and issues through content generation in local language;
- Need for a paradigm shift embodying the spirit of science, democracy and caring for the environment; and
- Promote positive environmental actions in pursuit of environmental and sustainable development goals.

ICT Integration

The Indian government has been quite optimistic in the promotion of ICT integration, particularly in school education over the last two decades or so. Some of the ICT Projects and Policies are reported to be of world standard. The government is collaborating with developed nations and other Global Economic Blocs for uniform ramification of ICT integration throughout the country and the state governments are also not behind the race as some of them have readily adopted the module for the benefit of the people.

Key Government Initiatives in a Nutshell

- **1994: DPEP**
  Computer aided education was initially introduced in India as an innovative activity under the District Primary Education Programme in 1994. ICT entered the education sector through DPEP, which spearheaded the design of the school information system.
- **2000: NCERT National Curriculum Framework for School Education**
  Providing access to global information sources was made a priority goal under the National Curriculum Framework for School Education released in 2000 by the National Council for Educational Research and Training (NCERT). (UNESCO Website (a); NCERT Website (a)).
- **2002-2007: The Tenth Plan Goals**
  The Tenth Plan outlined the goals of improving access and

reducing disparities within the Common School System, as well as:

1. Renewal of curricula with emphasis on vocationalisation and employment-oriented courses.
2. Expansion and diversification of the Open Learning system;
3. Reorganization of teacher training and greater use of ICT. (GOI, Ministry of Human Resource Development, Department of School Education and Literacy Website (c)).

- **ICT Smart Schools: The Tenth Plan**

  One of the important central government schemes formulated in the five year plan aiming at promoting the usage of ICT in government and government-aided schools (particularly in rural areas) and providing ICT infrastructure, addresses the four-fold components:

  1. Partnership with state governments and union territories for providing computer education and computer-aided education to government and government aided schools;
  2. Establishment of SMART schools as technology demonstrators;
  3. Universalisation of computer literacy through Kendriya Vidyalayas and neighbouring schools; and
  4. State Institutes of Educational Technology (SIET) to provide educational content in the form of films, videos, audios, etc.

- **2002: Vidya Vahini**

  In 2002, the Government of India launched a project called 'Vidya Vahini' to provide for IT and IT-enabled education in 60,000 schools in the country over three years (India has about 1.1 million schools), as part of Rs. 6,000 crore (USD 1.2. billion) project. Beginning with a pilot covering 150 schools, the government proposed to equip each school with a computer lab, equipped with Internet, Intranet and Television to facilitate video-conferencing, web-broadcasting and e-learning (Kumar, A., October 9, 2002).

- 2002: Technology Tools for Teaching and Training in India (Project T4)

In September 2002, the T4 project was launched in the states of Karnataka, Chhattisgarh and Jharkhand, and subsequently, in the state of Madhya Pradesh. The programme offers Interactive Radio Instruction (IRI) and educational television for mathematics, science and English as a second language and is designed to reach some of the hardest-to-reach populations (Funded by USAID, with collaboration of state governments and local organizations).

- **2004: EDUSAT**
  Launched in September 2004 at a cost of USD 20 million, Edusat is India's first education-dedicated satellite. With footprints covering the entire country, Edusat makes it possible to receive Direct to Home quality broadcasts of educational programme using any television set and a low-cost receiver. The result of a collaboration between the Indian Space Research Organization (ISRO) and the Union Ministry of Human Resource Development, State Departments of Education and the Indira Gandhi National Open University, this infrastructure is available to all sectors of education, but primarily to publicly funded and implementing agencies that will be responsible for the transmission and programming for their defined audiences (*lype*, July 28, 2005).
- **2004: Bridges to the Future Initiatives**
  This is a partnership initiative between the International Literacy Institute (ILI) at the University of Pennsylvania (USA) Byrraju Foundation, IIIT, and other agencies in the state of Andhra Pradesh. The programme aims at providing literacy programme in the local language to out-of-school youth and primary school students, using computer infrastructure in schools after school hours. The results of a two-year long impact study shows dramatic results in putting drop-out youth back into school, and raising the learning achievement of in-school children aged 8-10 years in poor rural settings (Wagner, Sridharan and Daswani, January 9, 2007).
- **2006: Broadband Connectivity in All Secondary Schools**

The Government of India, Ministry of HRD, the Department of Secondary and Higher Education issued an order for the constitution of an Integration Action Plan to implement Broadband connectivity in all secondary schools (Order dated May 20, 2006, GOI, HRD, Department of Secondary and Higher Education Website (e)).

- **2007: Digital Library and Information Network**
  Based on the recommendations made by different state open universities and distance education institutions (DEIs), the Indira Gandhi National Open University's (IGNOU) Board of management approved the National Open and Distance Learners' Library and Information Network (NODLINET) initiative. The expert committee set up by the Ministry for Human Resource Development (MHRD) endorsed the initiative to be implemented in a phased manner within a period of five years (*Times News Network*, April 22, 2007).

Mission 2007: Every Village, a Knowledge Centre

Mission 2007 proposed to establish 600,000 Village Resource Centres by August 15, 2007, coinciding with India's celebration of 60 years of independence (Swaminathan, M.S. November 25, 2006). Establishing connectivity and covering the 'last mile' are the imperatives of this ambitious plan under the schemes like National Knowledge Network (NKN); National Programme on Technology Enhanced Learning (NPTE); and National Mission on Education through ICT. To that end, Bharat Sanchar Nigam Limited (BSNL) has planned to connect 80,000 villages of India through wireless broadband.

2009: National Policy on ICT in School Education

The mission of ICT Policy in School Education is to devise, catalyse, support and sustain ICT and ICT-enabled activities and processes in order to improve access, quality and efficiency in the school system.

The government's role in this sector seems to be quite futuristic and effective with a set of world standard projects in hand. Information and Communication and Technology and e-learning are the medium of fast connectivity and development, showing a tremendous growth since 1990. The Government of India has launched policies and programmes for the smooth penetration of ICT at the grassroot level so that awareness can be generated at educational, social, economic and political domains for the benefit of the people. Domestic e-learning industry, about 10 per cent of the total industry size, has been experiencing a healthy CAGR of approximately 30 per cent over the last five years. The state governments have to initiate programmes related with e-learning and ICT for a smooth transition of information between the government and the people, thereby helping overall socio-economic development of the country

Conclusion

One of the most pressing concerns in the new millennium is the protection of the human habitat and the environment that nurtures it. Even as humanity moves towards the path of sustainable development, there is need for a paradigm shift in its approach to education. The path is undoubtedly fraught with challenges in spite of the Supreme Court of India directives and consequent curricular frameworks, which render EE as a compulsory component of syllabi at all levels of learning. In the context of teacher training, there is need to strengthen the existing programmes and reorient them to integrate ESD and EE in the curricular transactions. DEP-SSA can provide the training mechanism for teachers across the country through distance learning mode. Teacher educators at the State, district and block/cluster levels can operate in collaborative mode, thereby constituting the state/district resource group for the purpose. ICT can be harnessed to explore new possibilities to generate and share new knowledge in the area of EE.

8

Assessment and Evaluation

As per the Right to Education Act 2009, every child in the age group of 6-14 years shall be admitted in a neighbourhood school. All the identified Out-of-School children have to be enrolled/mainstreamed in the age-appropriate class and thereafter provided special training (long-term/short-term basis) in the NRSTCs, functioning in the formal school campus itself.

Pre-preparation for Assessment

But, how is these students' progress evaluated? In keeping with the idea of representing a continuum of proficiency, grade-II teachers take all the chapter books in their classroom and sort them into grade-level stacks: I-I (grade I, first semester), 1-2, 2-1, and so on, up to grade V. Then, they identify representative or marker books in each category to use for assessment. Once the books having been sorted by their difficulty levels, it becomes possible to document that children were reading increasingly difficult texts with understanding. Photocopied pages from the marker-books also help the parents see what teachers considered to be grade-level materials and provide them with concrete evidence of their child's progress. Given the mandates for student-level reporting under Chapter One, the state departments of education or test publishers could help develop similar systems on their own with sufficient standardization to ensure comparability across districts.

In the meantime, classroom teachers—preferably teams of teachers—are left to invent their own assessments for classroom use. In many schools, teachers are already working with portfolios and developing scoring criteria. The best procedure appears to be having grade-level teams and then cross-grade teams meet to discuss expectations and evaluation criteria. These conversations will be more productive if, for each dimension to be assessed, teachers collect student work and use marker-papers to illustrate the continuum of performance.

Also envisaged is a re-envisioning of assessment that recognises two principal functions of assessment: assessment *FOR learning*; and assessment *OF learning*, instead of the more familiar categories of formative, diagnostic, summative and evaluative assessment. The use of these two functions of assessment highlights and emphasises on the contribution that assessment can make to the day-to-day process of teaching and learning. Giving due weight to its role, it helps to create a cumulative record of children's progress and

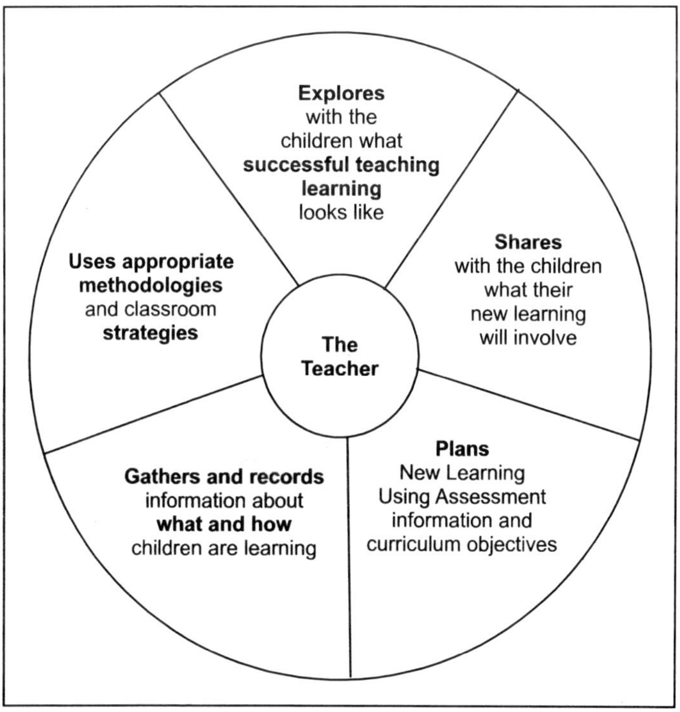

Figure 8.1: Assessment of the Teaching-Learning Cycle

attainment. This new categorisation does not replace the more familiar description of the functions of assessment; rather, it subsumes them into the new categorisation. The concepts of assessment *for* learning and assessment *of* learning help the teacher establish the degree to which the child has acquired a particular knowledge; understood particular concepts; or mastered certain skills and has identified the next step in learning to help the child engage in new learning in a successful way. This general theory of learning is reflected in the aims, principles and the defining features of the Primary School Curriculum.

Assessment for **Learning (AfL)**

The concept of assessment for learning (AfL) extends the potentials of formative assessment. It emphasises on the child's own active role in learning; in that teacher and the child agree on what should be the outcomes of learning and the criteria for judging the extent of outcomes achieved. In essence, AfL helps teachers and children to focus on three key questions:

- Where are children now in their learning?
- Where are children going in their learning?
- How will children get to the next point in their learning?

Providing feedback to children is central to AfL. It is based on the evidence of how and what the children are learning. Feedback focussed on the learning task in hand helps children identify and celebrate their progress and achievement; pinpoint challenges they experience; and decide what should be the next steps. This level of involvement in shaping their own learning can heighten children's awareness of themselves as learners and encourage them to take more personal responsibility for, and pride in, their learning. AfL does not generally happen at the end of a particular piece of work or a period of time. It usually takes place in the day-to-day minute-by-minute interactions between teachers and children. Everything that the children do, say and make—asking questions, working on a project or task alone or collaboratively, playing, designing or making a model, and so on—has the potential of providing the teacher and the children themselves with information about what they do and do not understand; and what they can and cannot do. Using AfL, the teacher interprets this information and uses it to support children in their work and to plan ahead. In this way, the teacher can integrate AfL into teacher-children interactions and children can come to regard it as a natural part of how they learn in the school.

The teacher can also use information from AfL to evaluate one's own teaching. Based on information gathered from children, the teacher can make relevant changes in planning, organisational strategies, and teaching methodologies to make learning more successful for children. Through assessment for learning, the teacher will gather continuous and extensive information about the children's progress and attainment through observing their performance in and engagement with the day-to-day learning activities in the classroom. In evaluating their response to the teacher's questions, the quality of their involvement in class and group activities and the counter-questions posed by them in the learning situation, the teacher can obtain a wealth of minute information in relation to individual children's learning. Tasks and tests undertaken both in the classroom and at home will be directly related to particular learning objectives, and will add a further dimension to the picture the teacher constructs of the progress of individual children. Correspondingly, portfolios, accumulated work samples and projects will provide information regarding the progress the child is making over a longer period, such as a month or a term. In using assessment for learning, the teacher takes account of all this information about every child's progress, attainment and possible areas of difficulty in providing regular and high quality feedback to the child and in planning for the future learning experiences.

Assessment for learning includes what is known as formative assessment of out-of-school primary children. It is wider in scope since it would include both diagnostic as well as evaluative assessment, too. No doubt, the term evaluative assessment is usually associated with the evaluation of schools and of educational systems. Based on this evaluative information, the teacher can make decision regarding content and infrastructural inputs, choice of appropriate teaching approaches and methodologies to be used for remedial teaching of the students

Finally, though the standardised tests are only one of the many assessment tools used to gather information about a child's progress, the limitations of standardised tests, for example, do not provide an absolute measure of the cultural bias inherent in test questions. It is important that outcomes of these tests and that of teacher-designed tests must be considered in the broader context of the student's overall performance and progress.

Entry-level Assessment Profile of Out-of-School Children

It is important that assessment be used to identify children with learning difficulties at the earliest possible stage to help them with appropriate support and to put in place apt interventions. Using appropriate tools would help teachers identify at-risk children. Diagnostic assessment has an important role to play in this process. It is not necessary to administer formal diagnostic tests to all children. Indeed, most teachers would not have the time to do this. Part of the school's assessment plan should detail the role of diagnostic assessment, including its place in the sequence of assessment procedures appropriate in identifying and addressing individual children's learning difficulties. Learning-Support Guidelines, issued by the DES, suggest an approach, which is as follows:

Learning-Support Guidelines

The class teacher should understand the nature and functions of diagnostic assessment and also be familiar with a range of formal and informal diagnostic tests. Entry-level assessment measures student's mastery of preceding sets of content standards. They serve as prerequisite building blocks for the forthcoming content. Typically, the prerequisite knowledge has been learned in preceding years or in separate courses. Entry-level assessment helps the teacher determine what, of the planned course of instruction, has already been mastered by students. Basic psychometric principles, as given below, must be followed for an entry-level assessment which could then be used reliably and effectively to compare their performance in the classroom (or school); or to establish a baseline to measure their growth. These principles are:

- Assessment must be administered under the same conditions to all students;
- Assessment must be administered using the same directions to all students; and
- Assessment must be scored in scaled increments, small enough, to detect growth to master content standards.

Types of Assessment

Two types of assessment supports AfL (Assessment *for* Learning) and AoL (Assessment *of* Learning) are: (1) Informal Assessment; and (2) Formal Assessment

I. Informal Assessment

Informal assessments are of the naturalistic assessment types and procedures take that place in the natural classroom environment during the typical early learning situations, making them more authentic than standardized testing, which must necessarily take place in a controlled setting outside the classroom.

Informal Assessment Tools and Methods

Informal assessment tools and methods include Anecdotal Records; Observation Schedules; Conversation Learning; Portfolio; Questions and Answers; Checklists, Rating Scales and, Rubrics; and Teacher-designed tasks and tests.

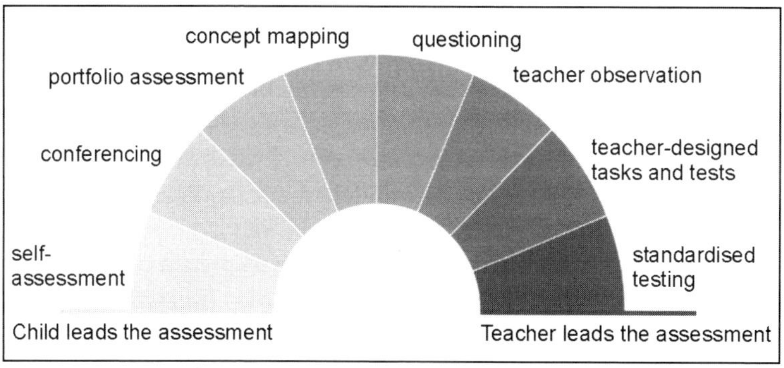

Figure 8.2: Assessment Methods

1. Anecdotal Records

Step 1: Taking Anecdotal Notes

Anecdotal notes are used to record specific observations of individual student behaviours, skills and attitudes as related to the outcomes of the programme of studies. Such notes provide cumulative information on students' learning and direction for further instruction. Anecdotal notes are often written as a result of ongoing observations during the lesson and also in response to a product or performance that the student has completed. They are brief, objective and focused on specific outcomes. Notes taken during or immediately following an activity are generally the most accurate. Anecdotal notes for a particular student can be periodically shared with the students or be shared at the students' request. They can also be shared with students and parents at parent-teacher-student conferences.

The objectives of taking anecdotal notes are to:

- Provide information regarding a student's development over a period of time;
- Provide ongoing records about individual instructional needs;
- Capture observations of significant behaviours that might otherwise be lost; and
- Provide ongoing documentation of learning that may be shared with students, parents and teachers.

Tips for Establishing Anecdotal Notes

1. Keep a binder with a separate page for each student. Record observations, using a clipboard and sticky notes. Write the date and the student's name on each sticky note. Following the note taking, place individual sticky notes on the page reserved for that student in the binder.
2. Keep a binder with dividers for each student and blank pages to jot down notes. The pages may be divided into three columns: Date, Observation and Action Plan.

3. Keep a class list in the front of the binder and check off each student's name as anecdotal notes are added to their section of the binder. This provides a quick reference of the students you have observed and how frequently you have observed them.
4. Keep notes brief and focused (usually not more than a few sentences or phrases).
5. Note the context and any comments or questions for follow-up.
6. Keep comments objective. Make specific comments about each student's strengths, especially after several observations have been recorded and a pattern has been observed.
7. Record as the observations are being made, or as soon after as possible, so that recollections will be accurate.
8. Record comments regularly, if possible.
9. Record at different times and during different activities to develop a balanced profile of student learning.
10. Review records frequently to ensure that notes are being made on each student regularly and summarize information related to trends in each student's learning.
11. Share anecdotal notes with students and parents at conferences.

Step 2: Maintaining Anecdotal Record

Whereas anecdotal records are the written observations—word for word, action for action—of exactly what a child is doing and saying; a transcript, if you will, on an event, series of events or even throughout the day. Anecdotal records have many benefits. The most important, if done accurately, is, that it is a true and an unbiased account of precisely what is occurring.

Format of Anecdotal Records with Examples at Primary Level

Example 1

Anecdotal Record

Setting Learning Centre
Activity: ____Table toys_________ Date: ____11/09/02__
Name: ______Akshit_______ Recorder: ____Tina (Teacher)______

Akshit ran over to the table where other students were completing puzzles shouting, "Here I come!" He then approached another student and asked, "Can I have that puzzle?" Other student: No. I have not yet finished. Akshit: But I need that one to build my rocketship. Other student: Mrs. Sarita says you have to wait for your turn. Akshit: Mrs. Sarita, can I have that puzzle now? Mrs. Sarita: when _he__ has finished, you may have a turn. Akshit: Set the timer then. (to other student). You have 1 minute; right, Mrs. Sarita? Akshit then sat at the table with his face supported by his hands and repeated cautions 5 times: 'Time is almost up'. When the timer rang, Akshit took the puzzle and dumped it and began assembling it himself.

Anyone reviewing this record can "see" exactly what occurred at the table. An anecdotal record should be written in a *positive tone*. It needs to emphasize what a child is doing and his or her *achievements* as opposed to what the child is not doing. There is no room for using biased observations or words in writing anecdotal records.

Example 2

Anecdotal records are written after an event has occurred. The observer uses memory to note significant events or actions, preferably within two days of the observation made to ensure the accuracy of information.

Student: Mohit **Age:** 6 years, 2 months
Observer: Rakesh Gupta **Date:** 7th July 2013, 11:45am
Setting: Classroom

Purpose

To observe Mohit's sentence-structure with peers.

Observational Question

Does Mohit use simple sentences or more complex sentences when interacting with his peers?

Observation Details

Mohit played with the drama materials for 15 minutes, using the dress-ups and examining himself in the mirror. He walked over to the home corner table and said to another boy, 'Hey, give me that.' He took the spoon from the other student. I spoke to Mohit and asked him to give the spoon back to the other student. He gave the spoon back and said, 'I like choc milk and a biscuit too!'

I asked the children to pack up. Another adult approached Mohit asking him to help pack up. Mohit replied to the adult, 'And then can we go outside?' The adult replied 'Yes! 'Mohit shouted 'Yay' and started packing up.

Analysis

Mohit was able to use both simple and complex sentence structures. He demonstrated confidence in his interactions with his peers. Mohit was able to engage in appropriate 'turn taking' during his brief conversation with an adult.

Example 3

It is Ten-thirty on Wednesday morning, October 12, 2012, in the Dino room at Grand Rapids Community College Preschool Laboratory. Liam, four-year old, is standing at a kidney shaped table with five other children and three different tubs of blocks. Liam watches the boy on his left pick up a block from the floor. Liam moves over to the block on the floor and tries to touch it with his foot. Liam returns to the table, he has a blue tubular block in his right hand. He says, "Whoa, watch this." and he begins to roll his block on the table and pushes it across the table. He runs around the table and retrieves the block. He takes his right hand with the block in it and pushes the train in the centre of the table to the side. Next, Liam returns to his original spot at the table and says, "Oh, watch this, watch this." He, then, rolls the tubular block again on the table. Liam looks at the boy next to him and smiles and rolls his block to the centre of the table again. This time, the block goes to the centre of the table and Liam reaches out with his right hand and retrieves the block. He repeats this motion with the block once more.

Guidelines for Writing Anecdotal Records

1. Observing Children—Anecdotal records tell a story as they describe behaviour, complete with verbal responses in a narrative style.
2. Writing Anecdotal Records—Start with a statement; setting, date, time of day, name and age of child. Describe the child's behaviour as observed, NOT what you think of the behaviour. Use details of the child's actions and comments, include others' responses;
3. Research Methods—When observing children, there are many research methods used to gain information, such as observations/anecdotal records, surveys and interviews, standardized tests, physiological measures, case studies, correlational research, experimental research, cross-sectional and longitudinal methods.
4. In Lab observations, assignments, you will be observing children using observations called anecdotal records.
5. Written observations of children in anecdotal records allow us to—assess development in all areas—physical, social, cognitive and emotional; learn more about the child as an individual; identify interests for the group and/or the individual; show progress and share information; assess the curriculum; and data to drive various decisions.
6. Write down the exact words used in the conversation; Most complete episodes have a beginning, middle and an end. Documenting this helps your understanding to be more complete.
7. Some things to remember about anecdotal records—Professionalism—Anecdotal records are confidential! The objective analysis is not the conclusion or diagnosis. It should not include any bias.

2. Observation Schedules

Observing students—as they solve problems, demonstrate skills to others, think aloud during a sequence of activities or interact with peers in different learning situations—provides an insight into their learning and growth. The teacher explores and examines questions like: Under what conditions success is most likely? What individual students do when they encounter difficulty? How interaction with others affects their learning and concentration? And what do they need to learn next? Observations may be informal or highly structured, and also incidental or scheduled over different periods of time in different learning contexts.

Observation schedules allow teachers to record information quickly about how students perform in relation to specific outcomes from the programme of studies. Observation checklists, written in a yes/no format, can be used to assist in observing student's performance relative to specific criteria. They may be directed toward observations of an individual or a group. These tools can also include spaces for brief comments, which provide additional information not captured in the checklist.

Before using an observation schedule ensure that students understand what information will be gathered; how it will be used; ensuring further that the checklists are dated to provide a record of observations over a period of time.

Tips for Using Observation Schedules

1. Determine specific outcomes to observe and assess.
2. Decide what to look for. Write down criteria or evidence that indicate that the student is demonstrating the outcome.
3. Ensure students know and understand what the criteria are.
4. Target your observation by selecting four to five students per class and one or two specific outcomes to observe.
5. Develop a data gathering system, such as a clipboard for anecdotal notes, a checklist or rubric, or a video or audio recorder.
6. Collect observations over a number of classes during a reporting period and look for patterns of performance.
7. Date all observations.
8. Share observations with students, both individually and in a group. Make the observations specific and describe how

this demonstrates or promotes thinking and learning. For example; "Eric, you contributed several ideas to your group's Top Ten list. You really helped your group finish their task within the time limit."

9. Use the information gathered from observation to enhance or modify future instruction.

Examples

Case-1

Ánnya is four and a half. Her teacher, Soniya, is concerned about her language development; in particular, her colour recognition skills. She plans to observe Ánnya and her best friend, Kavya, as they enjoy some free-play the following day. Soniya knows that they like dressing up, so she provides a lot of very colourful clothes for them to try on. Kavya picks a bright blue coat from the lot. She opens the buttons and puts on the coat. She closes the buttons carefully and admires herself in the mirror. "I like blue," she tells Ánnya, who is struggling with a fluffy pink jumper. Ánnya pulls the jumper over her head, but cannot get her arms into the sleeves. Soniya asks her if she needs help. "No," Ánnya, "I will do it myself." Kavya laughs and helps her to pull the jumper on the right way around. "What colour is your fluffy jumper?" Asks Soniya. "Its green," she says. "No," says Kavya, "your jumper is pink! We look pretty!" When her class has gone home, Soniya makes an entry in her folder on the classroom PC. She opens the file marked Kavya. Scrolling to the end of the document, she types:

Sample Teacher Record on Kavya October 21, 2012

Manages buttons well.
Knows the colours blue and pink.
Is helpful to her friends.
In Ánnya's file she types:

Sample Teacher Record on Ánnya October 21, 2012

Shows some language delay.

Needs help with dressing.
Not sure of colours pink or green.
Likes to do things independently.
Soniya saves the new information and closes the files.

Case-2

CLASSROOM OBSERVATION

Student: ___Priyanka________ **Age:** _4_______________

School/Centre: DAV Public School, Faridabad_ Anshu (Teacher)
Observer:_Anshu (Teacher)___________ **Date:**___1/01/13_____

Time of observation: _____9:00 am____ to ___9:30 am_____

____

Instructional setting:

_____ Classroom _X__ Small Group _____ Individual _____ Other

____

Behaviour Modification

Description of Activity

Priyanka has designated the block area as her choice of play and is building an apartment building with two other female classmates.

Description of Relevant Behaviours

To determine whether Priyanka is able to work cooperatively with others, it is noted that Priyanka negotiated on three separate occasions for a particular set of building materials, as given below:

1. Asked to use the arch block to create "the place people go in". When the other child declined, Priyanka asked to have it when she finished.
2. Another child asked Priyanka if she could "add on" to her

building. Priyanka agreed with the contingency that the buildings "not touch".

3. When transitioning to the next learning centre, Priyanka was about to leave without putting her building materials away. One of the children said, "Hey, you have to clean up too!", to which Priyanka responded, "OK." She then moved very slowly, but did pick up eight to ten blocks and placed them in proper bins before moving on.

Description of How Behaviour Impacts Functioning

The demonstrated behaviour leads the observer to determine that in a small group setting, Priyanka is able to work cooperatively with peers.

Signature: ___Anshu Teacher_______ Title: ___Lead teacher______

3. Learning Conversations

Conversations are particularly effective in helping students learn and make connections. There are a number of ways to keep track of learning conversations. For example:

- **Record the learning conversations by using an audio digital recording device.** Either the teacher or students can download the recording and use audio-editing software to identify the most salient parts of the conversation and add them to their portfolios.
- **Record the learning conversations by video.** Either the teacher or students can create the video recording and use video editing software to identify the most salient parts of the conversation and add them to their portfolios.
- **Record their emerging understandings, working theories, solutions and reflections through a classroom Website; e.g., chatroom, blog, wiki.** Students can then continue their conversations outside of school, build on each other's ideas, and have a rich record of how

their knowledge is built and how deep understanding emerges through open conversation.

4. Portfolios

- A portfolio is a collection of a child's work from very specific areas. Two advantages of portfolio assessment are: that it shows students' progress over time; and involves students themselves in the assessment process. Its drawbacks are equally noteworthy. It consumes a large amount of time to compile and that it is quite subjective in its nature. Like all informal assessments, portfolios too lack the elements of reliability and validity.
- A portfolio is a purposeful collection of students' work samples, students' self-assessments and goal statements that reflect their progress. Students generally choose the work samples to place in the portfolio; the teacher also recommends that specific work samples to be included. Portfolio serves as a powerful tool that allows students to see their academic progress from grade to grade.
- The physical structure of a portfolio refers to the actual arrangement of the work samples, which can be organized according to chronology, subject area, style or goal area. The conceptual structure refers to the teacher's goals for student learning. For example, the teacher may have students' complete self-assessment on a work sample and then set a goal for future learning. The work sample self-assessment and the goal sheet may be added to the portfolio.
- Work samples from all curricular areas can be selected and placed in a portfolio. These would include stories, tests and reflections about one's work samples.

Example

Ms. Sarita teaches fifth class and uses portfolios to assess the children's work in English during the year. She gets the children make their folders (A3 size) and design the covers. She tells the children at the outset that the purpose of the portfolio is to show others and themselves how their English work improves during the year. About every two weeks, Ms. Sarita gives the class some time to look at their pieces of work and asks them to select what they think is a good piece. On its back, they write one or two sentences explaining what is good about it. These features/qualities of good work are written on posters by Ms. Kennedy and displayed on the classroom wall magazines to help children refer to them and provide the basis for useful discussions.

Over the months, the collection of work in each portfolio grows. By the end of the year, each portfolio has about fifteen items including poems, pieces of writing (some descriptive and some in story form), the re-telling of news items discussed in class and accounts of holidays and school events. There are also word puzzles and quizzes, jokes and cartoon strips. Children store this portfolio on a shelf in the class library. Ms. Sarita is surprised at how well they look after their portfolios. At the end of the year, the class has a portfolio presentation whereby each child has a minute to talk to the class about the work tendered and select their best piece. Many of the children are able to say how their work in English improved over the year. The portfolios are of great interest to parents as well, as they are kept posted with their children's progress reports.

5. Questions and Answers

Questions, when related to outcomes, serve as assessment tools. Teachers use questioning (usually oral) to discover what students know and can do. Strategies for effective question and answer assessment include:

- Apply a wait time or 'no hands-up rule' to provide students with time to think after a question before they are called upon randomly to respond.
- Ask a variety of questions, including open-ended questions and those that require more than a right or wrong answer.
- Use Bloom's Taxonomy when developing questions to promote higher order thinking.

Teachers can record the results of questions and answers in anecdotal notes or include them as part of their planning to improve student learning

Example 1

Mr. Manish is teaching the topic of sound to twenty-two first and second class children. He starts with attention-focusing questions. He taps a spoon on the side of an empty jam-jar.

Mr. Manish: What sound can you hear? Is it a high sound or a low sound?
Pratham: It is a high sound.

Mr. Manish half fills the jam-jar with water and taps the jar again. This time he uses a comparison question.

Mr. Manish: Is the sound higher or lower than the last time?
Ashish: Lower!

Mr. Manish: What do you think will happen to the sound if more water is added to the jam-jar?

The children are invited to predict the outcome. This process is repeated a number of times adding more water or lessening water. When children are familiar with the possibilities of various levels of water in the jam-jars, Mr. Manish decides that they are now ready for problem-solving questions. He sets one group of six children a task of trying to compose a tune using only jam-jars and water. To another group of six children, he gives a selection of elastic bands and cardboard boxes. To the third group, he gives a variety of beaters (spoons, rulers and so on) and common classroom objects to investigate sounds made using different materials.

At the end of the activity, each group presents its findings, and Mr. Manish is able to assess what each member has learned using further questioning and observations.

Example 2: Probing Questions

Key Objectives Reception	Probing Questions
Say and use the number names in order in familiar contexts	• Can you count to 10? • What number comes before/after? • If I start at 3, can you count on/back? • Say a number rhyme. • Show the right amounts using fingers/other resources. • How do you know that there are only four ducks left? • Adapt for other rhymes and stories
Count reliably up to 10 everyday objects	• Can you find out how many x are needed for …? • How many drum beats can you hear? • Can you do five jumps? • How many cars can you see? • How can you count these ….? • Show me how to count …. • Give me/show me a group of five bears
Recognise numerals 1 to 9	• Can you put these numbers in order? • Can you count and then show me the number? • Can you give me number 5 from the washing line? • Can you show me number 3
Use language such as more or less, greater or smaller, to compare two numbers	• Can you make a number sentence to explain how much more/less there is or you have? • Can you change this amount of things and tell me how you have done it?

Key Objectives Reception	**Probing Questions**
	• Baseline link—which set has more/less? Can you tell by just looking? Can you explain why? • Show me the group that has more. How do you know it has more?
In practical activities and discussion: begin to use the vocabulary involved in adding and subtracting	• Can you solve a problem about numbers that is in words? e.g. 2 people on the bus, 3 more get on? How many? Explain it. • Cakes/something of child's interest, explain what add means ... give them a definition to learn. • Can you tell me what I am doing? (Teacher shows practically)
Find one more or one less than a number from 1 to 9	• Can you change this number to 1 more or 1 less? • Use a number line. • Sets of objects? • How do you know that the number is correct?
Begin to relate addition to combining two groups of objects	• Baseline link. • Show me how you would work out 2 add 1
Begin to relate subtraction to 'taking away'	• Make sure that it is actually 'taken away' from sight, e.g. a child saying "It's behind your back". • How do we/you know that there are 3 green bottles left?
Talk about, recognise and recreate simple patterns	• Threading beads by number of colours. • Explain why/thinking. • Copy patterns. • What would come next? How do you know?

Key Objectives Reception	Probing Questions
Use developing mathematical ideas and methods to solve practical problems	• Give us a clue … it has 4 legs, 2 legs, 8 legs etc … • which one is the odd-one-out … bike ↑ car ↓ van↓ • Was there anything to help you work out your answer? • How do you know your answer is correct?
Use language such as more or less, longer or shorter, heavier or lighter… to compare two quantities	• Assessment opportunity • Language coming out from weighing bears/etc. • Hand measuring • What did you use to find out ….? • How do you know ….?
Use language, such as circle or bigger to describe the shape and size of solids and flat shapes.	• How do you know this is a circle (in the feely bag), e.g., a square • Order smallest to biggest • Why have you used these words? • Tell me what a circle looks like?
Use everyday words to describe position	• Use a puppet to position/or an object on a picture/PE apparatus • Where is the …….? • Can you show me …….? • Can you put----- on------?

6. Checklists, Rating Scales and Rubrics

Checklists, rating scales and rubrics are tools to meet state-specific criteria. They allow teachers and students to gather information and make judgements about what students know and can do in relation to the outcomes. They offer systematic ways of collecting data about specific behaviours, knowledge and skills.

The quality of information acquired through the use of

checklists, rating scales and rubrics is highly dependent on the quality of the descriptors chosen for assessment. Their benefit is also dependent on students' direct involvement in the assessment and understanding of the feedback provided.

The objectives of checklists, rating scales and rubrics are to:

- Provide tools for systematic recording of observations;
- Provide tools for self-assessment;
- Provide samples of criteria for students prior to collecting and evaluating data on their work record, development of specific skills, strategies, attitudes and behaviours necessary for demonstrating learning; and
- Clarify students' instructional needs by presenting a record of current accomplishments.

Tips for Developing Checklists, Rating Scales and Rubrics

1. Use checklists, rating scales and rubrics in relation to outcomes and standards.
2. Use simple formats that can be understood by students and that will communicate information about student's learning to parents.
3. Ensure that the characteristics and descriptors listed are clear, specific and observable.
4. Encourage students to assist in constructing appropriate criteria. For example, what are the descriptors that demonstrate levels of performance in problem solving?
5. Ensure that checklists, rating scales and rubrics are dated to track the progress over time.
6. Leave space to record anecdotal notes or comments.
7. Use generic templates that become familiar to students and to which various descriptors can be added quickly, depending on the outcome(s) being assessed.
8. Provide guidance to students to use and create their own checklists, rating scales and rubrics for self-assessment purposes and as guidelines for goal setting.

Examples

Checklist Format: Science Process Skills

Criteria:	**1**	**2**	**3**
Makes detailed observations			
Looks for attributes			
Distinguishes inferences vs. observations			
Uses right measurement units			
Measures accurately			
Listens carefully			
Communicates clearly			
Classifies by attributes			
Recognizes patterns			
Makes predictions based on data			
Chooses correct graph			
Identifies manipulated/responding variable			
Controls variables			
Interprets results cautiously			

Problem-solving Rating Scale

1	3	5
I do not understand the problem		I can explain this problem
1	3	5
I cannot recognize the important and unimportant parts of this problem		I can recognize the important and unimportant parts of this problem
1	3	5
I do not know where to start		I can solve the problem & explain my solution
1	3	5
This was a difficult problem		This was an easy problem

Comments:

7. Teacher-designed Tasks and Tests

Tasks and tests can take the form of written or oral assessment or practical assignments developed by the teacher to assess children's learning. They can be used throughout the school year as a basis for continuous assessment (AfL). Tasks and tests can also be used at the end of an academic year or at the end of a period of learning about a certain topic for the purpose of AoL. However, tasks and tests can serve both AoL and AfL at the same time, since teachers may firstly report the results of tasks and tests and then use the results to decide what they should teach and how they should approach each topic.

What is the value of teacher-designed tasks and tests as an assessment method?

Tasks or tests provide opportunities for children to demonstrate their levels of understanding (or misunderstanding) and their skills, and offer valuable information that can be used to plan future work directed towards the children's needs. General guidelines for developing a teacher-designed paper and pencil test could be spelt out as below:

- Identify the purpose of the test at the outset and design the test to meet this purpose.
- Try to formulate questions, which relate to the children's own interests as this helps make the test relevant and motivating for children.
- Start with some easy questions that all the children can answer in order to help them overcome their nerves and feel confident that they can succeed.
- Include at least two types of problems in tests. When only one type of problem is contained on the page, children quickly pick up on this pattern; and it discourages them from reading and thinking about the problem. New problems can be mixed in with the ones that the children can solve already in order to provide opportunities for children to show different degrees of integration of knowledge and different levels of ability.
- As far as possible, write questions using a simple subject-verb-object-structure, even when this may result in more words being used.

For Example: Instead of Writing

Example A

Blue paint is added to a jam-jar containing yellow coloured water.

> The colour of the water changes.
> What colour does it become?
> The question could be phrased as:

Example B

Laura has a jam-jar containing yellow coloured water.

> She adds blue paint to the jam-jar.
> The colour of the water in the jam-jar changes.

What colour is it now?

Using a child's name, as in example B, also allows for the use of more simple, direct sentence structures.

- Avoid using double negatives in questions.
- Think about the overall layout of the test, and how the information will be presented. For example, a single question should be contained on one page to help children follow questions more easily.
- Give key information in bold. The use of pictures and labelled diagrams can help to make questions more accessible.
- Vary the questions so that they assess the children's reasoning skills behind their answers and the methods they use.

How are Teacher-designed Tasks Used?

Many teacher-designed tasks involve children working in small groups. For assessment purposes, a high level of interaction between the teacher and the group of children is recommended. In order for this to occur, the teacher may decide that it is necessary for just one group to work on the activity while the remaining children are engaged in other work that does not involve much input or supervision from the teacher.

Feedback on Tasks and Tests

Use of grades or external rewards such as stickers for feedback on tasks and tests is generally of limited help to children in AfL. The main purpose of providing feedback is to give information to children about where they achieved success in relation to the learning intentions and where they might improve. Children need time to read or talk about the feedback as well as time to make improvements based on it.

Example

Ms. Sheena is teaching a mixed first and second class group of twenty-five children. Building on the children's experience of sorting and matching, she begins the activity with the whole class on the carpet, looking at a collection of pictures of animals pinned to a display board. She asks the children to choose an odd-one-out and to give a reason for their choice. The pictures of animals are chosen to focus on particular vocabulary (for example, mammals, egg-layers, distinguishing characteristics of insects and so on). She notices that children find it easier to identify differences based on visual features, so she encourages them to articulate and explain what the corresponding similarities are. She designs a quick informal test involving differentiated activities to assess the children's thinking about the characteristics relevant to scientific classification.

This test provides children with opportunities to use specific vocabulary in a way that reveals their understanding of terms that are important for classification. For the younger and less able children in the class, she introduces a game called 'In the Ring'. The children work in pairs with a hoop for sorting and sets of cards with pictures of animals. She asks them to find farm animals and put them in the hoop. She asks questions about the animals in the hoop and those out of the hoop. Ms. Sheena then asks the children to take all the animals out and put other animals in the hoop (for example, animals that hibernate). She presents the older and more able children in the class with a grid (odd-one-out board) containing names of animals (see below).

Sample grid of animal names

Squirrel	Polar bear	Cow
Hedgehog	Penguin	Bat
Swallow	Butterfly	Hen

She asks the children to choose a row or a column and complete an odd-one-out template, recording the similarities and differences between the animals and then to pick the odd-one-out giving a reason for their choice.

II. Formal Modes of Evaluation of Learning of Out-of-School Children after Special Teaching

Standardised tests are most often associated with the summative aspect of assessment, or assessment of learning. This has tended to obscure their value in assessment for learning. The information gained from a child's performance on a standardised test will provide a measurement of the child's mastery of particular concepts and skills. In many cases, these may confirm the judgements the teacher has made on the basis of other forms of assessment evidence.

The value of standardised tests lies not just in their potential to quantify a child's performance. They can also provide information on the child's performance in specific aspects of learning, including individual test items. Some mathematical tests, for example, allow the teacher to document the performance of each pupil on each item. An-item-by-item analysis of a child's performance on standardised tests can sometimes enable the teacher to identify areas of a particular difficulty.

Moreover, an error analysis by the teacher of a child's incorrect responses can be particularly informative in illuminating the precise nature of a child's misunderstanding or difficulties. The teacher can then draw inferences about the content or processes to be emphasised in teaching and learning either for an individual child, or for a class or a smaller group.

Finally, it is important to note that the standardised test is only one of the many assessment tools used to gather information about a child's progress. A child's completed standardised test does not provide an absolute measure of his/her achievement. Standardised tests have their own limitations. For example, 'culture' bias inherent in test questions. It is important that the outcomes of these tests (and of teacher-designed tests) must be considered in the broader context of the student's overall performance and progress.

Relevance of Assessment Information

The assessment information, the teacher gains from various modes of assessment will be relevant both to assessment of learning and assessment for learning. Similarly, the records of assessment that the teacher makes for the purpose of assessment for learning will also be used in the assessment of learning. However, the two differ essentially in the purpose for which assessment is used. In recording assessment information for the purposes of assessment for learning, the teacher's focus is on using the assessment information gathered to provide ongoing feedback to the child and to plan learning experiences to meet his/her learning needs.

Assessment information in relation to the assessment of learning will, on the other hand, constitute a record of the child's progress and attainment whether at class or school level, at the end of a given period of learning, at the end of a unit of work, at the end of a term, or at the end of a year. It might, for example, involve any or all of the following activities:

- Reviewing a child's written work for a term, making an overall judgement according to agreed and specified criteria and assigning a grade;
- Administering a group-administered standardised test of reading and generating a standard score and percentile rank for each pupil; and
- Reviewing a child's portfolio of work for a year, making an overall judgement, and, after discussion with the child, assigning a grade.

Conclusion

Although both assessment for learning and assessment of learning will involve the recording of assessment information, the nature of the record and the language in which it is recorded will be quite different for each. A further defining feature of assessment of learning is that the assessment recorded for this purpose will form the basis for reporting to a variety of recipients, including parents, other teachers, other schools and other professionals associated with the education of the child. It is important, therefore, that the recording of such assessment information is consistent and readily communicable to such a varied audience. Although, as indicated earlier, summative records of achievement, such as standardised test scores or overall grades for a term or a year may be of some value in the context of assessment for learning, their primary value is in the area of assessment of learning.

Such assessment information should comprise a summative record of the child's progress and attainment together with relevant information pertinent to particular learning needs and characteristics of the child. Assessment and Information Communication Technology (ICT) has the potential to play an integral role both in the assessment of and assessment for learning. ICT is relevant to assessment in three particular areas, namely, the use of electronic portfolios in contributing to assessment; the use of ICT as an assessment tool, including diagnostic assessment; and the use of ICT for recording and analysing the results of assessment.

9

Innovative Practices in Teaching

"Children who learn together, learn to live together, so says the fourth pillar of education (Delors Commission, 1996, "Learning the Treasure Within," UNESCO).

The changing scenario for Innovative practices in teaching takes into consideration four developments as the nature of classroom composition is changing. The primary classes are grossing heterogeneous in terms of students' level of intelligence (in multiple senses), social diversity, economic imbalance (double disadvantaged learners), diverse interest and purpose of education. So also, the conventional pedagogic principles and practices that may not work effectively, thus, making room for the evolution of innovative pedagogy for the poor/disadvantaged.

Keeping this in view certain pedagogic innovations are being tried out and experimented in enhancing pupil learning, specially in the context of changing classrooms with an inclusive setting.

Traditional Practices

a) Learning Together

Learning together involves structuring classes around small groups that work together in such a way that each group member's success is dependent on the group's success. There are different kinds of groups for different situations, but all of them try to balance some key elements that distinguish learning together from competitive or individualistic learning.

Learning together can be contrasted with what it is not. It may not be having students sit side-by-side at the same table to talk with each other, as they do their individual assignments; not assigning a report to a group of students where one student does all the work and the others put their names on the product as well. It involves much more than being physically near other students, discussing material, helping, or sharing material with other students. There is a crucial difference between simply putting students into groups to learn and in structuring cooperative interdependence among them to learn together.

Extensive research has compared learning together with traditional classroom instruction using the same teacher, curriculum and assessments. On an average:

- Students, who engage themselves in learning together, learn significantly more, remember it longer, and develop better critical-thinking skills than their counterparts in traditional lecture classes.
- Students enjoy learning together more than the traditional lecture classes; they are more likely to attend classes and finish the course on time.
- Students readily go on to do jobs that require team work. It helps students develop the skills necessary to work on projects that are too difficult and complex for any one person to do in a reasonable amount of time.
- Learning together prepares students to assess outcomes by themselves.

b) Concept Networking

Concept Networking is a technique for representing knowledge in graphs as networks of concepts. Networks consist of nodes (points/verticals) and links (arcs/edges), nodes represent concepts and links are labeled. Links can be non-uni or bi-directional. Concepts and links may be categorized as simply associative, specified or divided in categories, such as causal or temporal relations. Concept networking can be done for several purposes, such as:

- To generate ideas (brainstorming, etc);
- To design a complex structure (long texts, hypermedia, large web sites, etc.);
- To communicate complex ideas;
- To aid leading by explicitly integrating new and old knowledge, and
- To assess understanding or diagnose misunderstanding.

The concept networking or mapping technique, developed by Prof. Joseph D. Novak of Cornell University in the 1960s, is based on the theories of David Asuble, who stressed the importance of prior knowledge in being able to learn about new concepts. According to Novak (1990), "Meaningful learning involves the assimilation of new concepts and propositions into existing cognitive structures."

Concepts, usually enclosed in circles or boxes of the same types, and relationships between concepts or propositions, are indicated by a connecting line between two concepts, words or the line, which specify the relationship between the two concepts.

A distinctive characteristic of concept networking maps is that the concepts are represented in a hierarchical pyramid fashion with the most inclusive, most general concepts at the top of the map and the more specific, less general concepts arranged hierarchically below. Its another important characteristic is the inclusion of "cross-links" indicating relationships (propositions) between concepts in different domains of the networking. Cross-links help to see how some domains of knowledge represented on the map are related to each other. A final feature that may be added to the concept maps is specific example of events or objects that help to clarify the meaning of a given concept.

c) *Peer Tutoring*

Peer tutor may be any one, who is of similar status as the person being tutored. Both the tutor and the tutee are from the same class. Peer tutor helps the peer tutee in the teaching-learning tasks in the classroom, establishing rapport easily as compared to the class teacher. Peer tutor is, however, not empowered to give grade or marks as is done by a teacher.

Peer tutoring may be of several kinds such as Wide Class Peer Tutoring (WCPT), Peer Asserted Learning Strategies (PALS), and Reciprocal Peer Tutoring (RPT).

Teacher trains the students to act both as tutor and tutee to act as a tutor. Peer tutoring programmes benefit from highly structural activities such as teacher-made material and lessons, flash cards, worksheets, etc. Continual monitoring and feedback from the teacher help students engaged in peer tutoring. Students receiving peer tutoring are engaged in active learning and not simply listening.

d) Soft Skills Strategies

Soft skills incorporate all aspects of generic skills that include the cognitive elements associated with non-academic skills. Soft skills are identified as the most critical skills in the current global job market, especially in the fast moving era of technology. The reorientation of education for sustainability relates the importance of the so-called “Soft skills” in a business term that refers to the cluster of business skills related to leadership, communication and decision-making. Soft skills are distinguished from hard skills, being less technical and more social: soft skills mostly have to do with how you communicate and interact with people. To teach soft skills needs an abundance of soft skills to begin with, because teaching in itself is a soft skill and with practice and patience, it becomes easy to teach soft skills to all types of learners, students or employees.

Based on recent research findings, the following seven soft skills have been identified and chosen to augment better quality education in all institutions of higher professional learning.

- Communicative skills;
- Thinking skills and problem-solving skills;
- Team-work force skills;
- Life-long learning and information management skills;
- Entrepreneurship skill;
- Ethics, moral and professionalism skills; and
- Leadership skills.

These skills do have some bearing on the teaching-learning processes at the school level too and can be practised with advantage at the elementary education level as well as at the higher level, though in a restricted way.

Emerging Practices

With shift from behaviourism to constructivism, the emerging trend is to shift from teacher-centred instruction to the learner-centred, with new and emerging pedagogies, mainly comprising reflective teaching, constructivist teaching and techno-pedagoy, briefly presented here.

a) Constructivist Teaching

Constructivist teaching is based on the belief that learning occurs as learners are actively involved in a process of meaning and knowledge construction as opposed to passively receiving information. Learners are the makers of meaning and knowledge. Constructivist teaching fosters critical thinking and creates motivated and independent learners.

A constructivist is a practitioner, who:

- Believes that all knowledge is constructed or invented by the learner;
- Involves learners in active manipulation of meanings, numbers and patterns;
- Believes that learning is non-linear;
- Provides students with the tools of empowerment: concepts, heuristic procedures, self-motivation and reflection; and
- Believes that leaning occurs most effectively through guided discovery, meaningful application and problem solving

By adhering to such an ideal, the facilitator subscribes to the purpose of being a guide, a purpose that fosters change; allows learners to progress at a pace indicative of experience, knowledge and interest; and supports growth in reflective thinking.

Jonassen (1991) found that many educators and cognitive psychologists have applied constructivism to the development of learning environments and from these applications he has isolated a set of design principles such as:

- Create real-world environments that employ the context in which learning is relevant;
- Focus on realistic approaches to solving real-world problems;
- The instructor to be a coach and analyser of the strategies used to solve the problems;
- Stress on conceptual interrelatedness, providing multiple representations or perspectives on the content;
- Instructional goals and objectives to be negotiated and not imposed;
- Evaluation to serve as a self-analysis tool;
- Provide tools and environments that help learners interpret the multiple perspectives of the world; and
- Learning be internally controlled and mediated by the learner.

b) Reflective Teaching

Reflective teaching means looking at what you do in the classroom, thinking about why you do it, and thinking about if it works as a process of self-observation and self-evaluation. By collecting information about what goes on in the classroom, and by analysing and evaluating this information, identify and explore own practices and underlying beliefs, which may then lead to changes and improvements in the teaching-learning process.

Reflective teaching is, therefore, a means of professional development, which begins in the classroom with questions like

- Which teaching model am I using?
- How does it apply in specific teaching situations?
- How well is it working?

Every instructor starts with an initial theory of language teaching and learning, based on personal experiences as a language learner and, in some cases, reading or training. In reflective practice, the teacher applies this theory in classroom practice, observes and reflects on the results and adapts the theory. The classroom, thus, becomes a kind of laboratory where the teacher can relate one's teaching theory to teaching practice.

The theory provides a unifying rationale for the activities that the instructor uses in the classroom; classroom observation and reflection enable the instructor to refine the theory and adjust teaching practice. Concepts that the teacher acquires through reading and professional development are absorbed into the theory and tested in the reflective practice cycle.

This cycle of theory building, practice and reflection continues throughout a teacher's career, as the teacher evaluates new experiences and tests new or adapted theories against them.

c) Techno-Pedagogy

Traditionally students in a classroom used to be simply silent spectators or mute audience. They would attend lectures, and the professor or teacher gave lectures only. As opposed to generating discussion, the students would sit and listen for the duration of the class time. The only competition for the professor was the students' own minds, which could wander freely, but were still self-contained. But now, students have a vibrant technology. Through this technology, they can access a world of information, talk with friends, watch videos (without sound), and so on. It is true, they'd have to be discreet about it—continually taking out and checking one's phone, for example, tending to be obvious and clear. Now most students have laptops, and they use them to take notes, and it is very easy for them to do other things on their laptops while taking notes or instead of taking notes with little indication to the professor that anything different is going on.

IBW Potentials and Teacher Competence

Technology exposure implies something far more than just having students develop skills in a particular technology. It includes almost all types of techniques and methods, such as: integration methods; lab protocol; developing technology skills; learning how to gather tutorials and learning materials from the Internet besides the use of interactive white boards as tools of techno-pedagogy, a technology made up of a computer connected to both a projector and a touch-sensitive board that presents the pictures projected from the computer, allowing for changes, and receiving input electronically or by touch. Numerous studies have shown that the use of IWB improves learning processes, specifically where the integration between the teacher's instruction style and the IWBs' potential enables meaningful instruction (Betcher & Lee, 2009). Students acknowledge that the use of IWB enhances motivation to learn, raises the level of concentration, improves behaviour, and enhances learning as a "fun" and as an innovative process. In order for teachers to be competent and effective users of IWBs within their teaching and learning programmes, there are two basic skill sets that they require, that is, they need to have basic level of IWB technical skills and know-how to operate the technology as well as be confident in this operation. Teachers also need to have competent ICT pedagogical skills and pre-service teachers need to be taught how does an IWB work as well as understand how to pedagogically apply these technologies in such a way as to enhance student learning in a big way.

10

Revamping Primary Schooling Initiatives in Action

The Segregation Syndrome

The Indian Education System has the responsibility to gear up, harness and develop young minds and their talents by the thousands with each passing year in this age of expanding knowledge and skills in every field of human activity within the four walls of the school and beyond, irrespective of region, rural versus urban population, high and low class categories, language barriers and much more. How can the system create incredible performers and cultivate their best interests that are good not only for individual growth, but also for the good of the community or society as a whole. Primary schooling forms the foundation of the super-structure of an education system in that the stronger the foundation in terms of content, communication and learning outcomes at the base level, the better would be the chances of building bridges for creating an incredible knowledge society that takes pride in learning ever on. In this digital world with massive information flows all around and social media inputs of all kinds, every child entering the school portal comes with many a learning nuance unknown to generations hithertofore. This tantamounts to believing that the system has not only to impart them education in skills in an adequate way, but also to help them grow with an open mind to absorb and assimilate experiences, if found to be good, for their schooling and if found to be contrary or contradictory, to discard them altogether as negative inputs.

A study in caste and literacy—Education of the Dalits (quoted in Singh, 2008, p. 216-17) deserves attention to highlight the impact of incision/excision in primary education; it states:

> *"The factual position on untouchability came out in a Report based on a survey of 565 villages in 11 States by a group called 'Aman Biradari'. The convener of the group, Harsh Mande, whose other associates were: Ghanshyam Shah, Sukhdeo Thorat, Satish Deshpande and Amita Baviskar, reported a brief summary of their findings in the* Hindustan Times *of August 15, 2006." It follows as:*
>
> "Children in the rural areas learn early the rules of the caste, even as their country races into the 21st century. It was found that 38 per cent of the Dalit children in government schools were made to sit separately. Twenty per cent of the Dalit children were not allowed to drink water from the same source as others. A shocking 27 per cent Dalits were prevented from entering Police Stations and 28.7 per cent were prevented from ration shops, 33 per cent health and social workers refuse to go to Dalit homes and 23.5 per cent did not get their letters delivered at their residence. Segregated sitting for Dalits was found in 29.5 per cent Panchayats. And, in 14.4 per cent villages, they were not allowed even entrance to a Panchayat building."
>
> "Dalit settlements are more often found segregated from the main village. Such traditions are repeated even by government departments, just as in Indira Avaas Vikas Yojana. NGOs too do not lag behind in this practice. In the post earthquake (2001) rehabilitation programme in Gujarat, the NGOs followed the government norms, i.e. segregation of the Dalits from non-Dalits."

The study concluded on a rather highly disappointing note:

> "With untouchability, thus, persisting unashamedly in state institutions, like schools and police stations, in public spaces like temples and shops, in farms and markets, and in homes and hearts, the Dalit still lives in India waiting hopelessly

and sometimes in anger for the long betrayed dawn of equality."

Fate of Inclusive Education: Such studies ought to prove to be eye-openers for the system that has been clamouring for education of all in an inclusive environ as a measure towards revamping the system of primary schooling for over a number of years, even though the ground realities are found to be entirely different. This moving account speaks volumes about the need for inclusive development through inclusive education as an important improvement measure. However, despite being empowered with a constitutional mandate to promote social justice, most institutions of the Indian State have still a long way to go to ameliorate the situation in view, particularly of the fact that untouchability continues to have a direct bearing on one's literacy and education. In such a situation, access to and equity in education remain only a dream for the millions of the excluded, let alone the education of the millions of other children with disabilities and many more other deprived sections of the society.

Quality Education Determinant: Quality education, in the process of development, has also somewhere taken a backseat. The concept of Quality includes two terms—Quality Enhancement and Quality Assurance. At the initial stage, quality enhancement measures are carried on by the budding institutions. No institution, even when it is at the budding stage, can be said to have zero quality. Therefore, it tries to enhance its quality measures. Later on, after a few years of its inception, the institution tries to provide quality assurance after having established itself and its standards. Quality is equated with the level of human resources and facilities. School effectiveness and learner achievement are treated as indicators of quality. Quality encompasses a wide range of factors in it. The quality of an institution must be understood in the 'context' of the institution itself. NCTE and NAAC have tried to lay down various parameters to help set some benchmarks for quality. How effective and realistic they have truly been, however, remains a big question. Broadly speaking, the criteria of quality of teacher education institutions involves: (i) curricular aspects; teaching, (ii) learning and evaluation, (iii) research, consultancy and extension; (iv) infrastructure and learning resources; (v) student support and progression; (vi) governance and leadership and (vii) innovative practices.

How far has the quality move succeeded over the last four decades or so continues to baffle not only the quality policy makers, but also the whole lot of stakeholders in the education system at all levels and in teacher education in particular, in its worst form. In that millions of teachers duly trained by teacher training institutions and colleges of education during the last twenty years or so are finding themselves locked against the blind wall of employment for no fault of theirs on the pretext of quality assurance, which seems to have simply backfired due to policy paralysis and superficial restrictions that prove to be counter-productive in a very great measure, creating an imbalance of all sorts in teacher manpower planning, a kind of parabolic paradox for the system as such, both at school as well as at higher levels of schooling. While the system stands to suffer from acute shortage of teachers in all disciplines at every level, on the one hand, the ever-increasing flood of unemployed teachers across the road in search of adequate employment has turned out to be a big stigma too deep for tears for the system, on the other. The so-called quality parameters stand to lose all their significance and import, as all efforts tend to have gone awry leading to every kind of malpractices, nepotism and corruption to shame the Nation with millions of its teachers standing burnt out on the roadside than in the education system as respected teachers.

Effective Schools: School Effectiveness is the determinant of good quality. Effective school is one in which students progress further than might be expected from consideration of its intakes. An effective school, thus, adds extra value to its students' outcomes in comparison to other schools serving similar intakes. It is essential to have consistency and stability in effectiveness for a school to be effective. More and more innovations and value-added approaches focusing on progress over time need to be done to increase school effectiveness. The central focus of school effectiveness concerns the idea that the "Schools Matter", that schools do have major effects upon children's development and 'Schools Do Make a Difference'. But is it really happening begets questioning of all sorts?

Based on research evidence, the following factors may promote school effectiveness:

- Professional leadership participative, firm and purposeful;
- Shared vision and goal that should have unity of purpose, consistency of practice, collegiality and collaboration;
- An orderly and attractive learning environment;
- Focus on teaching and learning with special emphasis on maximization of learning time, achievement-oriented and academic emphasis;
- Purposeful learning with efficient organization, clarity of purpose, structural learning and adaptive practice;
- High expectation environment, communication skills and intellectual challenge;
- Positive reinforcement—clear and fair discipline and encouraging atmosphere for feedback;
- Pupils' rights and responsibilities—efforts to raise the pupils' self-esteem, fixation of responsibility, etc.;
- Monitoring progress—monitoring pupil performance and evaluating school performance;
- Home-school partnership—parental involvement in children's learning; and
- Learning organization dedicated to school-based staff development.

Performing Teacher: A good teacher is an effective sailor of the ship of learning. An effective teacher results in effective school effectiveness. Earlier, the notion of the teacher as a good teacher was "An Ideal Teacher', then it changed to 'Good Teacher', then 'Effective Teacher', then came 'Competent Teacher' and now the notion of a 'Performing Teacher'. Teacher performance refers to the behaviour of teacher within the class, outside the class, but inside school, and beyond school. Performance is a result of teacher competency interacting with the school situation. It is defined as 'What the teacher does'? Teacher performance is a product of interaction between teacher characteristics and teaching situation. It is often used as a basis from which teacher effectiveness can be both logically and empirically inferred. Teaching, if defined for teacher performance is the task of a teacher performed for the development of the child.

Five major performance areas for teachers could be as follows:

- Classroom Performance—that includes teaching and learning processes; evaluation techniques and classroom management, computer aided teaching and learning;
- School-level Performance—that includes organization of morning assembly, elaboration of national, social and cultural events, participation in school-level management and organization of student panchayats;
- Performance in Out-of School Activities—that include such educational activities as field visits of learners, observation tours, community living, etc;
- Performance Related to Parental Contact and Cooperation—that includes such matters as enrolment and retention, regularity in attendance, discussing progress reports, improving quality of achievement, etc.; and
- Performance Related to Community Contact and Cooperation—that includes such issues as VEC work, joint celebration of certain events by the community, eliciting community support in the development of the school, etc.

Recent Initiatives

A number of recent initiatives taken in school education at elementary, secondary and primary stages, as mentioned hereunder, deserve special attention in teacher education.

- First at the elementary stage, ***Sarva Shiksha Abhiyan,*** aiming at great reform since the year 2001, focusing on all children from 6-14 year age-group to get free education got its legal status on 1st April 2010 by way of Right to Education Act under Article 21(A) of the Constitution. It took ten long yeas to grant it the legal status. Now children from 6-14 years have a right to education and simultaneously, it is the duty of the parents to send their children to school.
- Secondly, at the secondary school stage, the vocational education at +2 level particularly being quite weak, *Inclusive*

Education has been initiated in schools to cover all categories of children in school. Separate inclusive schools are also working to impart inclusive education effectively besides pedagogic innovations to cover special needs children in the common school through new techniques and system. So too, education for minority children in the secondary school system.

- Thirdly, with National Curriculum Framework 2005 and with the consequent NCERT textbooks came reforms in the examination system, keeping at tandem the methodology and examination system. ***With Continuous and Comprehensive Evaluation*** introduced recently, the teachers' role increased with CCE to make it holistic evaluation of the students in a continuous manner in order to give a boost to education for all and more so, to quality of life. Child's performance is assessed continuously throughout the session rather than on the long three-hour examination, where the child sometimes is not able to exhibit one's true caliber.
- Then at the teacher education level, with greater public-private partnership in place, a large number of self-financing institutions have opened during the last more than ten years, maybe, to strengthen the teacher education system in terms of quality and effectiveness. Their outcomes have yet to be gauged whether they are really at it.

Challenges

Revamping the school education is in process via many of the initiatives being taken in school education and teacher education even though there lie many challenges as well as chasms to bridge the galloping gaps that exist in the system as a whole.

- ICT being the essential need in today's time, it has not reached all schools yet. It is provided only in a few select private schools and is neglected largely in government schools, so also in most primary schools.
- In inclusive education, there is a dire need for strengthening

the pedagogic component. Although the provision for inclusive schools has been made, they are lacking in pedagogic component and thereby in quality. There can be positive change in the pedagogic component if there is change in the attitude of the teachers. Creativity and critical thinking have to be promoted since the beginning of the school education.

- Distance Education seems to be on a very big move. It needs reform. The National Institute of Open Schooling and Directorates of Distance Education need to be strengthened in every state with greater use of ICT techniques, like teleconferencing, videoconferencing, e-mail, etc. via better pupil-teacher contact to improve schooling.

Conclusion

While the system needs a change, those who impart it, too need a change of heart. All kinds of challenges can be removed and initiatives can be enhanced only if there is a 'Right Attitude'. Whereas the Indian Education system needs revitalization, the imparters too need to change and realize that each student has different abilities that need to be recognized and nurtured in time. Only positive attitude for change would develop the will to live together with uniformity and without any resistance. Broader outlook towards innovations would certainly help.

11

Role of ICT in School Education

Backdrop

Since the dawn of civilization, human beings have always been trying to excel in various fields to bring a better quality to life in different ways. With the advancement in science and technology for improving life conditions and with their increasing use, the world has now become a global village. Technological application in all walks of life has been a major concern for globalization. Its impact is also visible in education, especially in the area of teaching and learning and facilitating the making of knowledge learners. Realizing the importance of Media and Educational Technology in India, the **National Policy on Education** in its modified document – 1992 (Media and Educational Technology), states: "Modern communication technologies have the potential to bypass several stages and sequences in the process of development encountered in earlier decades. Both the constraints of time and distance at once become manageable. In order to avoid structural dualism, modern educational technology must reach out to the most distant areas and deprived sections of beneficiaries simultaneously with the comparative affluence and ready availability". Further, "Educational Technology will be employed in the spread of useful information, the training and retraining of teacher, to improve quality education, sharpen awareness of art and culture, inculcate abiding values, etc., both in the formal and non-formal sectors. Maximum use will be made of the available infrastructure."

Challenges Galore

The country engages nearly 60 lakh teachers spread over around 14.9 lakh schools (13.3 lakh Primary and Upper Primary and 1.6 lakh Secondary and Senior Secondary schools) to educate about 2,025 lakh children (*Source*: DISE Report 2010 by NUEPA and Educational Statistics at a Glance by MHRD, GOI 2008). The analysis of data on the growth of teacher education organizations in the country reveals that the number of these institutions has multiplied manifold, i.e., as on 31.03.2000, there were 2,051 such organizations and as on 31.03.2005, the figure was 4,550 (*Source*: NCTE-Annual Reports, 2000-2001 and 2004-2005). As on 01.01.2008, this figure was 9,031 with an intake of 8,93,194 teacher trainees. (*Source*: Annual Report, 2007-08 MHRD, GOI).

The orientation of teachers and teacher educators of such a huge system at regular intervals is always a challenging task. Covering all such teachers and teacher educators only through face-to-face training and orientation programmes is virtually impossible. The organization of orientation programmes through a cascade model, i.e., multi-tier training strategy (training of Key Resource Persons, Master Trainers, etc. at State, District, Block and Cluster level) may be one of the modalities for training and re-training of a large number of teachers and teacher educators of the country. Special Orientation of Primary School Teachers (SOPT) and Programme for Mass Orientation of School Teachers (PMOST) were organized through adopting the strategy of cascade mode. However, keeping in view the time consumed for training, transmission loss through such programmes (training through cascade mode) and the resource crunch within the states, training of teachers through distance mode (video and audio conferencing) was considered to be a better option.

Similarly, imparting quality education to a huge number of teacher trainees undergoing pre-service teacher education programme (NTT, JBT, B.Ed. B.Sc. Ed., M.Ed. etc.) has been a challenge before the nation as the largest democracy in the world. The worst, however, is that a training millions of already trained and duly qualified teachers at all levels are continuously being discarded through a kind of elimination process on the pretext of teacher eligibility tests (CTET) to get quality teachers where the pass percentage is sheer around 1.6 per cent as per the recent CTET result. Much more so, they have even yet to clear the Staff Selection Board Competition before being appointed as school teachers. Until they clear it, they will be on the roadside among the crowd of educated unemployed teachers yearning at the crossroad of their life to earn their living by any means. The hard fact, therefore, is that there are now only a few takers to join pre-service teacher training so much so that the challenge has become so alarming that the universities have started hunting students for their pre-service teacher training programmes through outsourcing agencies. Thus, no wise boy or girl seems to be readily available to be a teacher, fearing undue elimination terror of multiplicity of tests, mostly of dubious nature, in the selection of teachers, prone to very many poor manifestation.

Besides, many other challenges before teacher education, i.e., diverse geographical and socio-cultural conditions, multiplicity of language, explosion of knowledge (speed of knowledge updating), deliberate dearth of quality teachers, frequency of curriculum change, emphasis on rote learning approaches, alarming teacher-taught ratio, lack of motivating organizational climate, load of administrative work on teachers and teacher educators, etc. further hinder imparting quality education and making the teaching-learning process an interactive one. Also, education is becoming expensive day-by-day through factors like privatization and commercialization of education, all the while the 'earn and learn' culture is coming fast, besides the educational loans lobby getting active in quite a big way.

ICT Facilitation: As a bail out mechanism to this challenge, the National Curriculum Framework (NCF)-2005 states: "Judicious use of technology (Multimedia and ICT) can increase the reach of educational programmes, facilitate the management of the system, as well as help address specific learning needs and requirements of young learners, teachers and teacher educators. For instance, mass media can be used to support teacher training, facilitate classroom learning, and be used for advocacy. Possibilities of teaching and learning at varied paces, self-learning, dual modes of study, etc. could all benefit from the use of technology, particularly ICT. The increasing use of the Internet has enabled the sharing of information and provided space for debate and dialogue on diverse issues hitherto unavailable at such a scale. Technological innovations are also necessary for appropriate equipments and aids for meeting the learning requirements of children with special needs. What needs to be underscored is that technology could be integrated with the larger goals and processes of educational programmes rather than viewed in isolation or as an add-on. In this context, technological use that turns teachers and children into mere consumers and technology operators needs to be reviewed and discouraged. Interaction and intimacy are key to quality education, and this cannot be compromised as a principle in any curricular intervention." In a sense, the NCF-05 emphasizes a paradigm shift in respect of the entire process of education. NCF calls for a shift to leaner-centric ways (primacy of active learner), provide scope for variations in learners' needs, multiplicity of learners' exposures, and creation of citizens capable of reflective thinking and empowered participation in development.

Promises and Prospects

ICT is a mediator of learning as a component of the learning environment. While it is difficult to measure and directly demonstrate the impact of ICT in schools on learning, it may be possible to suggest plausible impacts by connecting ICT as a mediator with the theories of learning and strategies for providing learning opportunities.

There are four distinct characteristics of computer technology, which have clear implications for using computers in the classroom: logical programming; interactive control; graphics and audio output; and information processing. There are many ways to use these characteristics to support students and teachers in improving their learning outcomes and increasing productivity, i.e. by increasing learner motivation and engagement, by facilitating the acquisition of basic skills, and by enhancing teacher training. ICT also serves as a transformational tool which, when used appropriately, can promote shift to learner-centered environment. ICT can help education in a multipronged way as discussed below:

1. Investigating Reality and Building Knowledge: ICT allows students to investigate more thoroughly the real world. They can more readily access information sources outside the classroom and can use tools to analyse and interpret such information. Information may be accessed through online systems or through data logging systems. Technology allows them to receive feedback, refine their understanding, build new knowledge and transfer from school to outside environment.

2. Active Learning and Authentic Assessment: In many classroom situations, it is difficult to allow students to be sufficiently active as participants. Typically, students are often passive, spending a lot of time listening or reading. It is well known that students are more likely to be interested and attentive and will achieve a wider range of learning outcomes if they can be active, learning by doing (Reginald Gregoire inc. *et al.*, 1996). Their engagement with the curriculum will increase as they are afforded opportunities to create their own information and represent their own ideas (Riel, 1998). Computer software can be used to provide students with learning experiences where they are interacting with the computer system. Alternatively, the software may support activities where they interact with other people either in person or on-line (Riel, 1998). In all these cases, the student has more influence on the learning processes and the activities can be more responsive to the needs of the students. This facilitates better the development of conceptual frameworks by students to assist in deeper levels of learning.

3. Engaging Students by Motivation and Challenge: The interactive and multimedia nature of modern computer systems has provided the opportunity for software developers to create increasingly more stimulating features. Studies have found that students like to use computers and are likely to develop more positive attitudes towards their learning themselves when they use computers (Reginal Gregoire inc. *et al.*, 1996; Schacter, 1999). Computer systems do provide the opportunity to create a wide range of interesting learning experiences. This is likely to help maintain student interest and interest in a wider range of students (Cradeler & Bridgforth, 2002). The interactive and multimedia features within software can be used to help students grapple with concepts and ideas.

4. Providing Tools to Increase Student Productivity: In the past, students had to spend a lot of time doing repetitive, low level tasks, particularly involving writing, drawing and computation. While it may be necessary for students to develop these skills at some point, on most occasions, they are pre-requisite to some higher-level tasks. Unnecessary repetition of low-level tasks is inefficient, non-motivational and may obscure the real purpose of the learning activity. Many computer applications provide the tools to support students in quickly completing these lower-level tasks, so that they can focus on the main purpose of the activity. Word processor, graphics packages, database packages, spreadsheets and other software support the performance of students. The use of scaffolds and tools can help students to solve problems that may have previously been considered too difficult for them.

5. Providing Scaffolding to Support Higher Level Thinking: There is an increasing range of software tools, which can be used to support the development of higher level thinking skills, such as application, analysis and synthesis. Tools can be used to analyse data, present data, link data or information, present information in different formats, simulate environments and conditions, and support interactive communications. This allows teachers to consider providing a range of activities to assist students to become critical thinkers, designers and problem solvers. Computer systems provide a wider range of motivating situations in which students can develop and apply these higher level thinking skills and provide opportunities to develop 'deep knowledge'.

6. Increasing Learner Independence: Computer systems are increasingly being used to provide learning experiences when and where they are needed. This provides students with greater independence not only in terms of when and where they learn, but also what they teach (Cradler & Bridgoroth, 2002). It is not necessary for all students to do the same thing at the same time. Teachers may provide students with access to software, allowing students to select different learning experiences. The class does not have to be treated as one group. Individuals or groups of students may consider learning topics independent of the teacher.

7. Integrative Learning: ICT-enhanced learning promotes a thematic, integrative approach to teaching and learning. This approach eliminates artificial separation between different disciplines and between theory and practice that characterizes the traditional classroom approach.

8. Evaluative Learning: ICT-enhanced learning is student-directed and diagnostic. Unlike static text-or print-based educational technologies, ICT-enhanced learning recognizes that there are many different learning pathways and many different articulations of knowledge. ICT allows learners to explore and discover rather than merely listen and remember.

Modalities

- **Conventional Gadgets and Instructional Aids**: Including projective and non-projective aids like films, filmstrips, slides, transparencies, tapes, tape recorders, posters, charts, models, hash cards, comic strips, word games, phone, etc.
- **Conventional Radio and Television Broadcasting:** There are a number of educational radio and television programmes in India produced by different institutions, such as Central Institute of Educational Technology (CIET), State Institutes Educational Technology (SIETs), Audio Visual Research Centres (AVRCs), Educational Media Research Centres (EMRCs), Indira Gandhi National Open University (IGNOU), National Institute of Open Schooling (NIOS), Indian Institutes of Technology (IITs), NIPCID, etc. for broadcast at scheduled times daily all over the country through All India Radio (AIR), FM-Radio (educational channel), DD-I (National Television Channel), Gyan Darshan (Educational Television Channel) and so on, which tend to provide quality education to students of schools, colleges and higher education institutions in their own respective subjects and disciplines to cater to the needs of their target groups.
- **Interactive Radio and Television:** Used as methods of delivery and supporting education at a distance are distinguished by their ability to support immediate two-way communication among a group of learners and teachers (Chaudhery, 2006). Interactive radio and television resembles the conventional classroom transactions at a distance. Teachers can also ask questions to students and

can view what is happening at different learning centres from studio through telephone and TV screen. Similarly, students can participate in the live lessons by asking questions and by answering the teacher's questions at a distance. The system, thus, provides a virtual classroom where teacher and distant learners can interact in the same manner as in face-to-face classroom. Major advantages are their interactive capabilities and facilitation of immediate, simultaneous and sustained communication among the learners. Interactivity provides feedback to the learners on their performance in the acquisition of knowledge.

- **Exchange of Database:** Computers are networked for online data communication, out-sourcing of information and exchange of files. Data that need to be shared by different users can be stored and maintained at a global storage and users can be given access to it with their user-Id. Teachers and students can log on to the database of the universities/institutions and benefit from them in various ways, e.g. be informed about the latest in research, navigate through one information topic to another, have an online explanation of different topics. Online data communication supported by a network facility is not only a highly interactive mode of communication, but it also enables quicker transmission of information.
- **Teleconferencing (Audio Conferencing, Video Conferencing, and Computer Conferencing):** Teleconferencing is an effective medium of synchronous mode of electronic communication to provide learning experience in real time situation to a large number of participants positioned at different locations without withdrawing them from the workplaces/schools. Teleconferencing, where the audio medium is used as a two-way communication is known as audio-teleconferencing. In audio-conferencing, both teaching end and learning end use audio as the medium of communication. Video-conferencing is arranged by combining two-way video and audio media. Video conferencing increases the quality of interaction, because

both the teacher/expert and the students can see each other and can share their feelings and experiences. Computer conferencing is the most effective way of teleconferencing. With the help of hardware, information can be sent and received at the convenience both of teachers and the students with the use of computers. It combines both synchronous and asynchronous modes of communication. Computer conferencing can be text-based or full video-based (Panda and Khan, 2006). DEP-SSA and NCERT, IGNOU are continuously organizing teleconferencing on different pedagogical and contextual areas for teachers and teacher educators across the country throughout the year by using the EduSat network.

- **EduSat:** A specially designed portal for education launched in 2008 to promote the cause of school education in the country and beyond.
- **Web-**Based Education: The World Wide Web (WWW) has become one of the most popular delivery methods for distance learning programmes. The web has the ability to deliver multimedia materials, and this quality makes it highly suitable particularly for distance learning courses. An educational website can help learners to read, see, hear and interact with web-based information. A good web-based course allows learners to browse through the information by scrolling; see the relationship between chunks of information; upload and download information, etc.
- **Social Media Inputs:** Of late, social media portals and platforms have been extensively used for electioneering in the recent Lok Sabha elections not only for building public opinion, but also for educating the massive population of voters through social media tools, like twitter, youtube, facebook, mobile phone, etc. To choose the right candidate. social media has a very important role to play in formal, informal and non-formal education at individual as well as institutional levels of schooling.

References

Alternative and Innovative Education for out-of-school children. *(2013) Website: www.edudel.nic.in/ssa/7.pdfý Retrieved on June 25, 2013.*

Ambasht, N.K. (2012). Age appropriate admission under Right to Education Act: Policy implications. *The Journal of Governance, July, 2012.*

Duffy T., Jonassen D., Lowyck J. (1993), *Designing Constructivist Learning Environments*, Springer -Verlag.

Edusat Website Retrieved March 6, (2010) from: http://www.edusatindia.org/

Ernst and Young (2012). *Right to Education: the Role of Private Sectors.* Kolkata: Author.

Fiveyr/ 11th/11_v2/11th_vo12.pdf-accessed on Oct. 01, 2009).

GOI (2008), *"Eleventh Five Year Plan 2007-12 Vol. 11,* Social Sector", Planning Commission, Government of India, Oxford University Press, New Delhi. (Also available at—http://planningcommission.gov.in/plans/planrel/fiveyr/ 11th/11_v2/11th_vol2.pdf-accessed on Oct. 01, 2009).

_______ (2009), "*National Policy on Information and Communication Technology (ICT) in School Education*", Department of School Education and Literacy, Ministry of Human Resources Development, Government of India, New Delhi.

_______ (2009), "*National Policy on Information and Communication Technology (ICT) in School Education*", Department of School Education and Literacy, Ministry of Human Resources Development, Government of India, New Delhi.

_______ (2009a), "*India 2009—A Reference Annual*", Publications Division, Ministry of Information and Broadcasting, Government of India, New Delhi.

_______ (2010), Ministry of Human Resource Development, Department of Higher Education Website. Retrived March, 06, from http://www.education.nec.in//Natpol.asp.

_______ (2010), Ministry of Human Resource Development, Department of Higher Education Website. Retrieved March, 06, from http://www.education.nec.in//Natpol.asp.

Govt. of India, (2009) *Right to Education Act*, MHRD, New Delhi

International Labour Organization. *Education as an intervention strategy to eliminate and prevent child labour.* Consolidated Good Practices of the International Programme.

MHRD (2008), "*Outcome Budget*—Department of School Education and Literacy", Government of India, New Delhi.

______ (2011). Sarva Shiksha Abhiyan Framework for Implementation based on the Right of Children to Free and Compulsory Education Act, 2009. New Delhi: Author.

Milestones in Indian Education. http://www.education.nic.in/sector.asp# milestone

Ministry of Law and Justice (2009). Right of children to free and compulsory education act, 2009. The Gazette of India, No. 35 of 2009, New Delhi.

NCERT (2005) National Curriculum Framework. National Council of Educational Research and Training, New Delhi.

______ (2005) National Curriculum Framework. National Council of Educational Research and Training, New Delhi.

NCTE (2009) National Curriculum Framework for Teacher Education, NCTE, New Delhi.

Newhouse. (2002). The Impact of ICT on Learning and Teaching, *A Literature Review*, Western Australia Department of Education.

Niranjanaradhya and Kashyap, A. (2006). *The 'Fundamentals' of the Fundamental Right to Education in India*. Bangalore: UNESCO and Action Aid India.

Patra, R. (2007). *Out of school children the 'abhiyan' to bring them to school*. New Delhi: EdCIL.

Perraton, H., Robinson, B. and Creed, C. (eds.) (2007). International Case Studies of Teacher Education at a Distance (Studien und Berichte der Arbeitsstelle Fernstudienforschung der Carl von Ossietzky Universität Oldenburg). Vol. 12. Center for Distance Education, Carl von Ossietzky University: Oldenburg, Germany.

SCERT, (2012) *Implementation of RTE, 2009-Challenges and Remedies*, 2012 New Delhi.

Singh, R.P. (2008). "*Regional Imbalances in Educational Development*", in Prakash, V. and Biswal, K. Perspectives on Education and Development: Revisiting Education Commission and After. NEUPA and SHIPRA, New Delhi, pp. 216-217.

Singh, L.C. (2008), quoted in '*Caste and Literacy-Education of the Dalits*', pp. 216-17.

Yashpal Committee Report (1993) *Learning Without Burden*. MHRD, GOI. New Delhi